painting
modernism

SUNY series in

LATIN AMERICAN AND IBERIAN THOUGHT AND CULTURE

Jorge J. E. Gracia and

Rosemary Geisdorfer Feal, editors

painting modernism

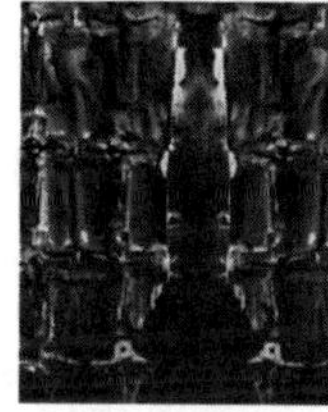

Ivan A. Schulman

state university of new york press

Cover art: *Theoretical Icon* (detail) from Duplicitous Icons series by John Michael Rusnak; 10 ft x 8.37 ft; abstract photography composed of India ink and stencil with overprinting on fiber based paper; 2011. Used by permission

Published by
STATE UNIVERSITY OF NEW YORK PRESS
Albany

For information, contact
State University of New York Press
www.sunypress.edu

Production, Laurie Searl
Marketing, Kate McDonnell

Library of Congress Cataloging-in-Publication Data

Schulman, Ivan A.
    Painting modernism / Ivan A. Schulman.
        pages cm. — (SUNY series in Latin American and Iberian Thought and Culture)
    Includes bibliographical references and index.
    ISBN 978-1-4384-4951-7 (hardcover : alk. paper)
    1. Modernism (Literature)—Latin America.   2. Art and literature—Latin America.   I. Title.
    PQ6073.M6S34 2013
    860.9'112—dc23   2013006240

To JMR, "vaso comunicante" illuminating the path of creativity

To MPG, to whom I owe my dedication to
the study of Latin American modernism

If I could say it in words, there would be no reason to paint.
—EDWARD HOPPER

Hay mucho de pintura en la poesía,
y hay mucho de poesía en la pintura . . .
—RUBÉN DARÍO

CONTENTS

INTRODUCTION

This book deals with a major aspect of Latin American modernism that canonical criticism has neglected to examine in its various dimensions.[1] The chapters of *Painting Modernism* are constructed upon the fundamental notion that literary texts should no longer be studied in isolation from other artistic discourses and that as a consequence we need to (re)examine the works generated by the writers affiliated with Latin American modernism, whose textual production transcends the limits of language and verbal imagery, or as David Scott has noted in chronicling the early history of "writing the arts":

> . . . inter-art correspondences . . . [are] predicated in part on a new concept of the artist, one that implie[s] the widening of the term to include the writer and the musician on the same footing as the painter and sculptor. (66)

We also are guided by the notion that "seeing comes before words"[2] and that it is "seeing which establishes our place in the surrounding world; we explain that world with words, but words can never undo the fact that we are surrounded by it."[3]

In the chapters that follow we use the term *modernism* in its broadest multidimensional implications, overriding traditional conceptualizations that both in the past and present view its texts as nothing more than aesthetic and escapist creations belonging to a period between 1888 and 1916.[4] As we have indicated elsewhere,[5] modernism's texts are both literary and social, and they are tied to the advent of Latin America's socioeconomic modernization; its writers, either consciously or unconsciously, responded in similar but fundamentally different ways to the new sociocultural order created by this process in texts that appeared as early as

1875 and as late as the second and third decades of the twentieth century. Modernism revisited today in the light of contemporary revisionist scholarship contains what we have referred to as "secret genealogies"[6] tied to a revisioning of its texts, one that is posited on the notion that modernism needs to be understood as an early manifestation of the notion of textual instability, an inconstancy that Baudelaire expressed early on in his essay "The Painter of Modern Life" (Ward and Patty, 18). Thus envisioned, Latin American modernism—indeed Western modernism—contains cadences and multidimensional fluctuations both in its aesthetic as well as its ideological dimensions; its writers responded to the social and political developments that transformed their function in society and the nature of their art in a variety of different manners but with the common denominator of experimentations that included, among others, internalizations, retextualized appropriations of the past, the incorporation of techniques borrowed from the sister arts of painting and music, and the search for spiritual meaning in an age of increasing materialism and industrialization tied to the incipient stages of capitalist society.[7]

José Martí (Cuba, 1853–1895), one of modernism's earliest literary theorists—and one of its principal writers—described the lack of constancy of these new-age transformations and the literary productions they produced, which he was instrumental in creating,[8] in the following manner: "There are no permanent works because the texts that belong to periods of realignment and restructuring are in essence mutable and turbulent: there are no set paths, new altars, broad and open as forests, are not yet visible . . ." (No hay obra permanente, porque las obras de los tiempos de reenquiciamiento y remolde son por esencia mudables e inquietas; no hay caminos constantes, vislúbranse apenas los altares nuevos . . .) (Martí 1963–1978, 7: 225]).[9] As a consequence, it is fallacious to view modernism as a school with prescribed or fixed modes of writing; its textual manifestations are multiple, heterological. Moreover, a rereading of the prose and poetry of this modern period of experimental literature reestablishes foundational links to subsequent postmodernist art. Its texts are a reflection of the openness, instability, ambiguity, and chaos of the metamorphic sociopolitical institutions of the modern world—West and East.

Latin American modernism—which spans both the latter half of the nineteenth century and the first half of the twentieth—is characterized, as we and other contemporary critics see it, by a pluralistic imaginary, and in that sense it is similar to the notion of the multiple existential philosophies of the twentieth century; and its texts are connected to elitist as well as to popular culture. In short, what we are suggesting, and what we hope will be evident in the chapters of this book, is that we subscribe to a revisionist notion of the nature and development of modernism that eschews micro in favor of macro discursive conceptualizations and produces a discourse that is visionary, not only in the traditional verbal sense but also in its links to plastic, especially painterly, associations.

Traditional critical discourse has preferred to emphasize a normative modernism viewed in terms of self-referentiality, fragmentation, elitist or escapist concepts, as well as subjective notions of cultural and aesthetic authenticity. The modernists' literary art, especially their epistemological search for the meaning of the modern world's new realities, has been described as an existential or teleological anguish conditioned more by emotional desperation than by a desire to understand in a rational way the ambiguous signs of nature and the reorganization of modernization's social structures. But modernism's aesthetic and social codes generated a literature that needs to be understood as a disconnect with the philosophical underpinnings of the Age of Reason or, in general, with Platonic, hierarchical structures. In the work of poets such as Rubén Darío (Nicaragua, 1867–1916), for example, there is a representative, constant search for individual and collective meaning, an attempt, colored by an underlying pessimism, to understand the restructured modernist world: "There are two gods; they are Ignorance and Oblivion" (Dos dioses hay, y son: Ignorancia y Olvido ["¡Ay, Triste del que un día . . ."]); or, "and not to know where we are going, nor from whence we came" (¡y no saber adónde vamos, / ni de dónde venimos! . . . ["Lo fatal"]).[10] In examining modernity, Paul de Man, reflecting upon this very epistemological question, writes that "the question of modernity reveals the paradoxical nature of a structure that makes lyric poetry into an enigma which never stops asking for the unreachable answer to its own riddle" (quoted in Ward and Patty, 186).

It is undeniable that the modernist imaginary demonstrates the presence of a personally based existential angst and a lack of reasoned hierarchical order. Nevertheless, it is still possible to discern generational commonalities among these writers as we hope to demonstrate in the pages that follow. In studying the interconnectivity of modernism's discourses, in particular the union of the plastic and verbal arts, our focus will be on the confluence of codes, visualizing them in the form of two intersecting circles, one represented by the individual text and the other by the social text. In short, we will examine the works of art discussed in this book as products of subjectively generated social/artistic practices inseparable, however, from socioeconomic transformations and the chaotic cultural crises of the modern world.[11]

The earliest manifestations of modernist writing belong to what might be termed the *first stage* in an arch of development that bridges the end of the nineteenth century and spans the first decades of the twentieth. In the second half of the nineteenth century the Latin American nations—especially those with more fully developed economies and urban centers—witnessed the inception of industrial movements. And with the arrival of a new market-based economic order—slow in growth and developmentally uneven in the various corners of the continent—a materialistic culture grew up that affected all social and cultural activities, including the nature of literary texts. The colonial system of patronage fell into disuse; writers and their works were "commodified" within a new marketplace system, their national stature was reduced, and the prominence they previously enjoyed during the vice royal and early Independence period (1820–1830) ultimately vanished. As a consequence, in this era of profound social transformation the writers' sense of social displacement, alienation, and personal anguish intensified. Three hundred years of colonial structures disappeared *de jure*, but in point of fact they remained operational in the postcolonial period, creating conflicting ideological positions among artists and intellectuals.

The rise of radically new, modernist imaginaries was bedeviled by the persistence of inherited colonial essences, a fusion that created a uniquely hybrid mind-set. Hybridity generated new linguistic codes and revolutionary discourses as early as 1875, reflecting the social structures and ideologies ushered in by modernization. Zavala tells us that the resulting literary texts inscribed a "master narrative" of decolonization and anti-imperialism (8). However, because of the cross-currents of hybridity, a doubleness of textuality resulted: two discourses at variance with each other surfaced. In one, the writers inscribed the signs of the rising power of the new bourgeoisie, that is, the hegemonic signs of mercantilism and industrialization that characterized the incipient modernization process. In the second, the search for cultural authenticity and self-sufficiency was voiced in a discourse of liberation from the dominant discourse of modernization whose icons of wealth, luxury, and European (principally French) refinement were, nevertheless, inscribed—consciously and/or unconsciously—in a counterdiscourse. In other words, the modernist counterdiscourse, which was tied to a long-standing cultural search for the expression of the voice of the Other, failed to erase the materialistic registers of the new dominant social discourse, and thus, in the majority of cases, their search for the liberation Zavala described went unrealized. In fact, most were not fully conscious of the conflictive nature of their discourse. Darío, for example in his "Palabras liminares," a prologue to his *Prosas profanas* (1896; 1950–1953, 5: 761–764),[12] described for his readers the prototypical confused discursive signs found in the texts of so many modernists:

> Is there a drop of African, Chorotega or Nagrandano blood in my veins? Perhaps, in spite of my hands worthy of a marquis; thus in my poetry you will see princesses, kings, things imperial, visions of distant or impossible countries: what can I say!, I detest the life and the time in which I was fated to be born . . .

> (¿Hay en mi sangre alguna gota de sangre de Africa, o de indio chorotega o nagrandano? Pudiera ser, a despecho de mis manos de marqués; mas he aquí que vereis en mis versos princesas, reyes, cosas imperiales, visiones de países lejanos o imposibles: ¡qué quereis!, yo detesto la vida y el tiemo en que me tocó nacer . . .) (1950–1953, 5: 762–763)[13]

Wavering in his discursive practice between Latin America (the blood drops in his veins), Europe, aristocracy, and the Orient, Darío's remarks perpetuated the textual enunciations visible in Latin American works from the colonial period forward—that is, a syncretistic, amphibolous discourse that melded the imposed values of the conquered and the voice of the Other's countercultural desires. And to this plurality the modernists added revolutionary stylistic practices that marked their production as distinct from the routine, tired academic premodern literary practices of the Hispanic world.

The syncretistic art of the modernists assumed a variety of styles. But one of its more obvious manifestations was the appropriation of the objects of (European) luxury collected by the members of the local oligarchies, including what the French Parnassians termed *noble, hard* sculptural materials such as gold, marble, or diamonds. In creating a new literary expression, they were particularly influenced by the European impressionist and expressionist painters and in some instances by the Japanese colorists. The resulting aesthetic expressions or ideological positions often constituted a contradiction in aspirations—typical of modern and postmodern literature—that is, the search for a native, authentic literature was mediated by the incorporation of exogenous discourses and aesthetic practices. The opposite was also operative for a number of modernists: their hybrid discourse refracted the objects and voices or the philosophical stances of the new materialistic hegemony while at the same time expressing a discourse of otherness that was critical of the center of power and revealed a resentment of marginalization characteristic of peripheral cultures and marginalized classes. In their search for a new discursive medium, they appropriated the products associated with the overseas expansion of the first stages of capitalism, that is, they imported (i.e., visually) objects from Europe, Africa, and the Orient, exotic objects that populate the works, for example, of José Asunción Silva (Colombia, 1865–1896), Julián del Casal (Cuba, 1863–1893), Rubén Darío, José Juan Tablada (Mexico, 1871–1945), and José Martí, as we shall see in the chapters that follow. For all of the foregoing reasons in examining the multiple discourses and "situational utterances" (Zavala, 20) of the modernists—especially the manner in which they appropriated the practices of painting, drawing, sculpture, or music—our fundamental position will be that modernism was never a purely "specular" movement or style, never wholly aesthetic or ideological, but rather a literature that attempted to expand its horizons in an age of modernization, a revolutionary postcolonial expression that paralleled Latin America's growing maturity and its disconformity with the social and political structures of the past and the social practices they reflected.

The past, however, was never rejected entirely, but when absorbed in modernist literature it was retextualized, illustrating the fact that these writers sensed that their inherited universes needed to be transformed—revisited. The past rematerialized became part of a modernized discourse whose emancipatory energies sought a collective transformation. The imperative of change was dictated by a reflective self-appraisal described by Martí in 1891: "we were a mask, he wrote, [with] the chest of an athlete, the hands of a dandy, and the forehead of a child. We were a whole fancy dress ball, in English trousers, a Parisian waistcoat, a North American overcoat, and a Spanish bullfighter's hat" (2002, 293).[14]

With all of these discordant and conflicting identities linked to a long-standing colonial mentality, the modernist writers intensified their efforts to (re)define themselves in a consciously autochthonous manner in both their sociopolitical as well as literary texts. Their nominal political liberation from Spain marked their entrance into the Age of Modernity.[15] It also marked the onset of the periphery's revisionist confrontation with itself—a double-sided undertaking that resulted in the deconstruction of the hierarchical universe imposed by the metropolis. In its struggle to construct an alternate universe, it decentered the foundations of its previous epistemologies, which in turn thrust the newly formed Latin American nations—and its writers—in the direction of an abyss of vacuity that ultimately produced a Dionysian counterdiscourse in place of the discourses of the premodern periods. The existence of a counterdiscourse, however, was not entirely new to the Age of Modernity; it existed previously in embedded voices of subaltern subversions during the colonial periods, but it surfaced and blossomed with the advent of modernism.[16]

The creative strategies of the modernists were diverse in nature. As Martí noted in his essay on Juan Pérez Bonalde, it was each person's task to reconstruct his or her life by looking inward (1963–1978, 7: 230). It was an existential search each writer assumed. Sacrosanct literary concepts were placed in question and a plurality of styles of writing was generated. The texts produced revealed psychological soundings, prophetic musings, aesthetic experiments, and philosophic explorations of the emptiness and alienation that was the consequence of the writers' marginalization in an age of materialism and postcolonial anguish. In modernist texts there is often lush imagery; abundant and unusual use of adjectives, an inclination toward linguistic transgression in the form of synesthesia, the brushstrokes of color and light, mythological figures, neologisms, and metaphors that reflect the new technologies and medical sciences of the late nineteenth century. There are texts in which blue princesses, gnomes, Venus, and Nirvana appear; and prose and poetry in which objects of marble, bronze, gold, silver, porcelain, and crystal are described with exquisite delicacy. But there is another side to the modernist discourse: compositions in which there are ideological and philosophical musings, texts that examine sociopolitical questions, texts that defend the need for political and economic liberation. Both discursive modalities are political in nature—even those that in surface readings appear to evade reality—because they are countercultural, critical of the new social and economic order. Both reflect and are a response to the spiritual nihilism of their age. Both, beneath their textual surfaces, contain an interiorized dialogue of liberation, a protest in the face of the often unjust, inhuman, and unacceptable conventions of modern society.[17]

❧

In chapter 1 we examine the nature of the modernist's search for new styles of expression that connect the discourses of the nineteenth century with vanguard twentieth-century texts and, ultimately, with contemporary postmodernist literature. There is a constant disconnection in their work with academic and traditional forms of writing, a movement away from conventional, realistic literature and the use of color and light, as well as other painterly techniques.

In chapter 2 we examine the painted narrations of José Martí, Efrén Rebolledo, and José Asunción Silva, who in diverse ways exemplify the transfer of plastic, musical, and cinematic techniques to the modernist novel.

Chapter 3 probes in detail the process by which a canvas is transformed verbally, transferred and retextualized in poetry, using as the incipient point a painting of the French artist Jean-Léon Gérome.

Chapter 4 explores the influence of the Orient, especially the work of its artists, in the writings of Enrique Gómez Carrillo, Julio Herrera y Reissig, Julián del Casal, José Martí, and José Juan Tablada.

In chapter 5 we study the art criticism of three Latin American modernists—Martí, Darío, and Tablada and the European and Oriental painters who captivated their imagination.

And finally, in chapter 6, we examine the visual poetry of Vicente Huidobro, who with his calligrammes takes the leap of moving words into the realm of visual objects.

In the construction of this book we draw upon a number of modernist writers whose exemplary visualizations constitute iconic illustrations of the application of the plastic arts to experimental verbalizations. We also draw upon the work of a number of influential Western and Oriental painters such as Gauguin, Gustave Moreau, Jean-Léon Gérome, Rubens, Goya, Raimundo de Madrazo, Velázquez, Fortuny, Vasily Vereshchagin, Hokusai, Hiroshige, and Utamaro.

In the chapters that follow we have been guided by the principle of *selectivity* rather than *inclusivity*. We are aware that the work of other modernists might have been examined with equal success. But, our overriding concern is to study the multiple, previously neglected dimensions of Latin America's literary modernization, which we hope to have illustrated with a select group of major nineteenth- and twentieth-century writers.

1

CROSSING BOUNDARIES

The Search for a New Discourse

NEW VENTURES

Contemporary (re)readings of modernism's texts as well as the examination of its principal writers' theoretical enunciations will substantiate our affirmation that among the Latin American modernists there existed a major interest in discovering and developing creative ties between literary art and the practices of late nineteenth-century and early twentieth-century painting and sculpture. From 1875 forward, Latin American writers were attracted to the unprecedented succession of innovations in pictorial and graphic arts, both European and Oriental.[1] Photography was invented in 1839, and Western writers, including those in Latin America, were immediately drawn to the creative possibilities of the new medium; their work also suffered the influence of the transition in Europe from academic painting to the art of the Pre-Raphaelites, impressionists, and later to that of the expressionists. Modernists in Latin America became obsessed with the notion of innovative visualizations, whether with the human eye or that of the camera. What resulted were aesthetic and stylistic experiments that created a new universe of textualizations based upon the "gaze."[2] Writers began to see the world as a picture; they set about writing with the lines and colors of canvases, sculpting statuesque lines, or re-creating with words what they had seen in art museums, reproductions, or photographs of contemporary plastic arts. In addition, the sound of music was subjected to a process of visualization and then transformed into vignettes—impressionistic or expressionistic in quality—and endowed with sensuous images, colors, and lines. However, "what distinguished the modernist literary

1

response from its predecessors stems from a crisis of belief in the continuity between seeing and knowing, and a commensurate cognizance of the subjective mediations of embodied visuality" (Jacobs, 19).

Writers internalized the world in order to perceive it more fully, understand its hidden nature—a generational undertaking that led to the construction of "alternative" realities and to the exploration of the nature of the Other. Painters posited the reverse, that is, they conceived of their art as a form of writing. Picasso, for example, considered that his prints constituted a form of writing. His lithographs and drypoints were for him a form of "writing fiction."[3] For Martí visualization preceded the act of writing: "I need to see beforehand—he wrote—what I intend to write" (Necesito ver antes lo que he de escribir) (1936–1953, 52: 128). And in his first volume of poetry (*Ismaelillo*, 1882), dedicated to his absent young son, he wrote in the prologue: "I have *painted* you exactly as you appeared before my eyes. Whenever I've ceased *seeing* your shape, I've stopped *painting* you" (16: 17; emphasis mine). In this same volume he dreams "with . . . eyes / open and always, by day / . . . always I *see*, floating, / a child, who calls to me!" ("Waking dream," 2002, 52; emphasis mine). On the one hand this volume of poetry proposes a revolutionary form of writing in its use of visual techniques, chromatics, and inventive metaphors, while on the other it preserves and retextualizes traditional Hispanic meters (pentasyllables, hexasyllables, and heptasyllables), demonstrating the fundamental nature of modernism's hybridity, a discursive quality described in the introduction.

Ismaelillo strikes a counterdiscursive note in the development of modernism.[4] The traditional "eye" or "gaze" of the poet deconstructs "rational" spatiality; in its place a subjective universe is substituted, one that first has been internalized and subsequently recast much as European expressionist painters re-visioned material reality and then externalized their emotional reaction to it in the form of a concrete but wholly individually perceived perspective and field of vision.[5] In Martí's poems traditional spatiality is absent; space is reorganized, landscapes become *inscapes*: "*You float over everything! / Son of my soul!*" (2002, 54, emphasis mine); ". . . red plumes move / Internal birds" ("Fragrant Arms," 16: 23); "From my dreams I drop down, / They disappear flying" ("Mischievous Muse," 16: 27); or "Minute eagles / Cover the air: / They are ideas, that rise, / Their prisons shattered!" ("Mischievous Muse," 16: 29)—all of these are fragments of lines that flow throughout this revolutionary book of poetry. Chaos—born of the structures and contradictions of modernity in its initial phases—invades and pervades the aesthetic space of *Ismaelillo*, a volume published in New York shortly after the poet's arrival there in 1880. Its tone reflects Martí's consternation at the pace of a modernized culture so different from the slower dynamics of life in the nations where the poet had lived or visited—Cuba, Mexico, Guatemala, Venezuela, Spain. He is fascinated, amazed, energized by what he sees and hears, but at the same time he is terrified by his gaze of life in New York City and along the Eastern seaboard, where he traveled by rail and ferry to organize the Cuban Revolution among Cuban émigré groups and tobacco workers. His first words in the introduction are: "My son: Frightened by everything, I take refuge in you. I have faith in human improvement, future existence, in the utility of virtue, and in you" (Hijo: Espantado de todo, me refugio en ti. Tengo fe en el mejoramiento humano, en la vida futura, en la utilidad de la virtud, y en ti) (16: 17).

Martí is not the only modernist who developed a frenetic interpretation of the incipient modern world and its attendant sense of loneliness and isolation that foreshadows the advent of twentieth-century nihilism and existentialism. Thrown into the marketplace of the early stages of American capitalism, writers in Latin America—including those who had never visited the United States—suffered a sense of displacement and angst. To deal with the loss of self generated by the Age of Modernity, writers like Martí focused their gaze inward in order to find the strength to overturn the fortunes of the world, cope with their social isolation, and attempt to redefine their identity:

> Man's first task [wrote Martí] is to reconquer himself. It is urgent that men be returned to themselves and extricated from the bad government of convention that suffocates or poisons their sentiments, accelerates the awakening of their senses, and overtaxes their intelligence with a pernicious, alien, cold, and false material wealth. Only what is genuine is fruitful. Only what is direct is powerful. What another bequeaths us is like a warmed-over meal. *It is up to each man to reconstruct life, and no sooner does he look inside himself then he reconstructs it.* (Prologue to "Poem of Niagara," 2002, 49; emphasis mine)

In the process of this reconstruction, visuality is a constant. It also dominates Martí's last volume of poetry, *Versos sencillos* (Simple verses), in which the poet moves about, unfettered in space, and links visions of his poetic discourse with that of all of the arts, with all the sites of nature:

> I come from all places
> And to all places go:
> *I am art among the arts*
> *And mountains among mountains.* (2002, 273; emphasis mine)

In discussing the primacy of the visual in modernist literature, Martí wrote in 1882 that

> [Today] there is no painter who succeeds in coloring the luminous aureoles of virgins with the novelty and transparency of other times. . . . There are no permanent works, because works produced during times of realignment and restructuring [generated by the Age of Modernity] are mutable and turbulent in their very essence: there are no set paths . . .
>
> (No hay pintor que acierte a colorear con la novedad y transparencia de otros tiempos. . . . No hay obra permanente, porque las obras de los tiempos de reenquiciamiento y remolde son por esencia mudables e inquietas; no hay caminos constantes . . .) (1963–1978, 7: 225)

The rejection of established norms, styles, and schools of writing gave way to an age of experimentation, to the introduction of what was later—in the twentieth century—characterized as vanguard literature but which had its roots in the modernists' early experiments. The colors of the artist's palette became a norm in the construction of literary texts. The influence of the French Parnassians was major in this endeavor, especially their interest in the introduction of plastic values in prose and poetry, in the invention of verbalizations capable of creating line and form in the manner of the painterly or sculptural arts. Texts such as Théophile Gautier's *Symphonie en blanc majeur* (1852) inspired similar creations in Latin America. Baudelaire's sonnet "Correspondances" (1857) followed with its concept of synesthesia—that is the intimate relationship the French poet perceived between sound and color. Other French writers proposed similar or even more daring notions: Rimbaud's "Voyelles" (1871) and René Ghil's *Traité du verbe* (1886–1888) linked visual perception to music and chromatics. These experiments prompted the Latin American writers to extend their interest in the aesthetics of color to visualizations produced by or connected to sounds. The fusion of the two senses resulted in the expression of new intellectual or emotional realities, new discursive ventures that enriched the modernist's verbal palette. In these new departures Martí was a trailblazer: as early as 1881, clearly inspired by both Ghil and Rimbaud,[6] he wrote:

> Between colors and sound there is a significant relationship. The cornet produces yellow sounds; the flute usually has blue and orange sounds; the bassoon and violin give off chestnut and Prussian blue sounds, and silence, which is the absence of sound, is black. White is the sound of the oboe.

> (Entre los colores y los sonidos hay una gran relación. El cornetín de piston produce sonidos amarillos; la flauta suele tener sonidos azules y anaranjados; el fagot y el violin dan sonidos de color de castaña y azul de Prusia, y el silencio, que es la ausencia de los sonidos el color negro. El blanco lo produce el oboe.) (1963–1973, 23: 125)

Other modernists focused their attention on the symbolic meaning of a single color. In his poem "De blanco" (On white), Manuel Gutiérrez Nájera, through the medium of metaphors, evoked suggestive meanings of the color white:

> What is whiter than a candid lily?
> What is more pure than a mystic candle?
> What is whiter than a tender orange blossom?
> What more virginal than a light mist?
> What more sacred than the divine altar of a
>   Gothic cathedral?

> (¿Qué cosa más blanca que cándido lirio?
> ¿Qué cosa más pura que místico cirio?
> ¿Qué cosa más casta que tierno azahar?
> ¿Qué cosa más virgen que leve neblina?
> ¿Qué cosa más santa que el ara divina
>   de gótico altar?) (Garfield and Schulman, 46)

Pictorial elements, music, symbolic colorings of an externalized previously internalized expressionistic gaze produced poems such as José Juan Tablada's "Ballad of the Eyes" ("Balada de los Ojos"):

> During the minuet, beneath the white lace
> I saw your red heel shine . . .
> Ah, Scarlatti's sonata
> Celebrated your sweet eyes!
>
> . . . .
>
> Watteau, Boucher, Fragonard, Greuze,[7]
> Each with their flirtatious brush
> Copied roses in your laughter
> And blue lilies in your eyes!
>
> . . . .
>
> (En el minueto, entre las blondas
> Miré lucir tu talón rojo . . .
> ¡Ah, la sonata de Scarlatti
> que celebró tus dulces ojos!
>
> . . . .
>
> Watteau, Boucher, Fragonard, Greuze,
> Con su pincel galante todos,
> Copiaron rosas en tus risas
> ¡y azules lirios en tus ojos!) (1971, 192–193)

OLD VENTURES REINVENTED: *UT PICTORA POESIS*[8]

Other modernists in their mind's eye captured visualizations in the form of paintings that they transferred verbally to prose, poems, or prose poems. Ekphrasis[9] became a favored discursive technique, which writers such as Rubén Darío used with flair in his early seminal modernist volume *Azul . . .* (Blue . . .) (1888), especially in the section entitled "En Chile" (In Chile). Krieger, in establishing the theoretical base for ekphrasis, states that

> . . . words cannot have capacity, cannot be capacious because they have literally no space. Ekphrasis involves a desire—since Plato—a romantic quest to attain a pre-fallen language of corporeal presence, using language as we know it to attain the magical transformation. (10)

Darío's painterly interests were related to his interest, shared by almost every Latin American modernist, in expanding the boundaries of linguistic discourse through heretofore untried plastic techniques. The sections of "En Chile" abound in luminous, chromatic expressions that in their time constituted aesthetic transgressions that nevertheless were not entirely original with the modernists.[10]

In the fourth section of "En Chile," "La Virgen de la Paloma," Darío alludes openly to the idea of painting in relation to literature and notes that he feels certain that in the hands of an accomplished artist this vignette could be a painting of signal artistic value: "I am convinced [he writes in a note,] that *this small 'watercolor' if treated by a painter of talent* would result in a work of art of signal aesthetic value" (1992, 129; emphasis mine).[11] It is clear from this note that Darío is aware of the technique of ekphrasis as he strives to redefine linguistic representation through the incorporation of new artistic techniques and enunciations. This process of hybrid textual construction is consciously manipulated in what might be termed the *introit* of this section of Darío's *Azul . . .* , in which the narrator asserts that Ricardo, a lyrical poet, seeks to create impressions, *canvases* he says, but *without brushes, palettes, paper or pencil* (sin pinceles, sin paleta, sin pincel, sin lapis) (125). It is more than possible, as Lida suggests, that Darío's early and constant French readings (53) led the author of *Azul . . .* to experiment with ekphrastic techniques whose optical values, given the form with which Darió endows them, reveal a hybridity characterized by an aesthetic intentionality combined with a political message: Ricardo, the instrument the narrator uses to express what might be termed *enargeia lingüística*,[12] seeks to flee from a commodified environment:

> the bustle and restlessness, of the engines and the bales, the monotonous noise of the streetcars and the clatter of the horses with their peal on the cobblestones; the bands of merchants; the daily shouting of the street vendors; the incessant noise and restlessness of this port . . .

> (las agitaciones y turbulencias, de las máquinas y de los fardos, del ruido monótono de los tranvías y el chocar de los caballos con su repiqueteo sobre las piedras; del tropel de los comerciantes; del grito de los vendedores de diarios; del incesante bullicio e inacabable hervor de este Puerto . . .) (125)[13]

The flight from the urban scene with its bustling commercial and industrial activity is emblematic of the sense of alienation experienced by the modernists faced with the transformations of economic modernization during

the first stages of capitalism. The writers of this first period living in major
cities felt trapped, displaced, and asphyxiated by the new socioeconomic
order; many sought the refuge of rural nature, other spaces, or the alternative universes of previous historical ages. Conscious of the changes associated with modernity, Martí, for example, in his analysis of the art forms
available to the modern writer, theorized that "the poem [for the new gen-
eration] exists in nature" (el poema [está] en la naturaleza) (1963–1978, 7:
229). And Ricardo, Darío's lyrical poet, echoing Martí's sentiments, focuses
his gaze on the battles and solemnities of nature, and, in a metaphorical
statement, envisioned an idealized "beautiful garden, with more roses than
azaleas and more violets than roses" (bello jardín, con más rosas que azaleas
y más violetas que rosas) ("Acuarela," 126). In Darío's bucolic painting that
bears the title *Watercolor*—and in which he moves from urban reality to
idealized nature—there is, on the one hand, a clear rejection of the materialistic culture of the second half of the nineteenth century and the desire
to find an antimodern refuge.[14] And on the other hand, we find a search
for the new in the elaboration of a pictorial vanguard aesthetic, a desire
to create in fiction what Praz termed, "some of the same formal liberties
and absence of conventional justification that prevail in modern pictorial
style" (192). Hence the titles of almost all the ekphrastic "vignettes" of "En
Chile": "Watercolor" (twice), "Landscape," "Portrait," "A Watteau Painting," "Still Life," "Pastel," "Charcoal."

Ricardo's flight from the city to the bucolic garden is as symbolic as
the painted landscapes. There is in these "literary canvases" an imaginary
geography of heights that constitutes an unmistakable metaphoric affirmation of the continuous search in early modernist letters for transition-
ing to an ideal Platonic or Pythagorean universe. Ricardo, the inveterate
dreamer, the narrator tells us, had reached the highest point of the hill
where the movements below could barely be perceived, where there was
sun and darkness and where he was thinking of idylls, with all the august
cheek of a millionaire poet (1992, 126). In the imagined spatial elements
of his vignette, Darío expresses the conflicted dualism of materialism/spiri-
tualism characteristic of the modernist writer's angst. Martí refers to these
very same conflicted feelings through a set of paired images of heights and
depths:

> There are mountains—he writes—next to abysses, and near
> infirmities, strength: tenderness and enthusiasm look toward
> the sky, and we see the poet *not in the depths whose gaze we dis-
> dain*, but in the mountain that witnesses our admiration.

(Hay montañas al lado de los abismos, y del lado de los decai-
mientos, fortalezas: el cariño y el entusiasmo miran siempre al
cielo, y nosotros vemos al poeta, *no en el abismo cuyo examen
desdeñamos*, sino en la montaña que presencia nuestra admi-
ración.) (1936–1953, 50: 190; emphasis mine)

The modernists searched the horizons for alternatives to the status
quo; their longings for release or change were expressed through trans-
gressive, often daring discursive practices. Like Martí, Darío painted with
words; he created what Lida has described in his study of Darío's prose as
an art of color and lines with an interplay of light and pictorial composition reminiscent of a painter's arrangement of inanimate objects (58). The
eye of the writer/painter is evident in "A Watteau Portrait" ("Un retrato
de Watteau," 1992, 132–133), a short narrative in which the eighteenth
century past is blended with modern times: it is a retextualized portrait in
the style of the aristocratic past in which the subject is a contemporary
aristocratic Chilean woman decked out for a ball and described by Darío
in a style worthy of Watteau's brush: "Dressed and adorned as the great
Watteau would have conceived her with his brushes" (vestida y adornada
como el gran Watteau la hubiera concebido con sus pinceles) (133). In
this prose poem Darío employs a variety of descriptive techniques that evidence his conscious desire to surmount the limitations of traditional nineteenth-century verbal practice. The initial scene is theatrical: the narrator
opens the curtain to present to the reader the mysteries of the dressing
room. Words translate visions; the narrator provides stage directions: "You
see the arm of the nymph, her tiny arms . . ." (Estáis viendo ese brazo de
ninfa, esas manos diminutas . . .) (132); "look," he says, "you see" (mirad;
vese) (133). Her waist, her skirt, her foot, the red heels of her shoes, are
described as in a painting (133). The narrator's gaze conjures up a setting
reminiscent of Velázquez's *Las Meninas*: the nymph looks at herself in the
mirrors of her dressing room as the eyes of a mythological Diana examine
her from the vantage point of her pedestal (133). Darío paints and sculpts
the objects of the room:

A statue of Diana, irresistible and nude elevated on her pedestal [examines her]; and a bronze satyr who bears a candela-
bra among the tendrils of his head laughs at her, and from the
handle of a Rouen pitcher of perfumed water, a siren with a
curved tail and brilliant silver scales extends her hands and
bosom . . .

> (Una Diana que se alza irresistible y desnuda sobre su plinto
> [la contempla]; y le ríe con audacia un sátiro de bronce que
> sostiene entre los pámpanos de su cabeza un candelabro; y en el
> ansa de un jarrón de Rouen lleno de agua perfumada, le tiende
> los brazos y los pechos una sirena con la cola corva y brillante
> de escamas argentinas . . .) (133)

In "La cabeza" (The head) in lieu of sculptural enunciations color is blended with langage as the narrator paints his text. Darío first read Martí's "luminous" prose during his stay in Chile;[15] and it was Martí who first theorized about the links between inspiration, ocular perception, color, and the art of writing: "Every painting [wrote the Cuban] has the color tones appropriate to it; because there are delicate tones such as pink or gray. . . . Blue requires rapid and vibrant accents, and black dark and spacious" (Cada cuadro lleva las voces del color que le está bien; porque hay voces tenues, que son como el rosado o el gris. . . . Lo azul quiere unos acentos rápidos y vibrantes, y lo negro otros dilatados y oscuros) (1992, 12: 187). In this same line of ekphrastic narration, the narrator of "La cabeza" describes the head of Ricardo, the poet of "En Chile," as "an orgy of colors and sounds. . . . And the colors, grouped together, were like petals of individual buds mixed together in a tray, or as *the diabolical mix of hues that fill a painter's palette* . . ." (una orgía de colores y sonidos. . . . Y los colores agrupados, estaban como pétalos de capullos distintos confundidos en una bandeja, o como *la endiablada mezcla de tintas que llena la paleta de un pintor* . . .) (1992, 130–131; emphasis mine).

The experimentation in "Acuarela" (Watercolor) is different. In this vignette Darío creates a "painting transfer"—but the base of his narrative is not a painting he might have viewed in a museum, but rather one that is the product of his imagination that then he endows with colors and lines:

> Here's the painting. In the foreground are the black colors of
> the carriages that shine and break up the last reflections of the
> sun; the proud horses with the luster of their harnesses, with
> the stiff and immobile necks of heraldic beasts . . . and seated
> in the rear of the carriages like odalisques, erect like queens,
> the fair women with dreamy eyes, black hair and pale faces . . .

> (He aquí el cuadro, En primer término está la negrura de los
> coches que esplende y quiebra los últimos reflejos solares; los

> caballos orgullosos con el brillo de sus arneses, con sus cuellos
> estirados e inmóviles de brutos heráldicos . . . y en el fondo de
> los carruajes, reclinadas como odaliscas, erguidas como reinas,
> las mujeres rubias de los ojos soñadores, las que tienen cabelle-
> ras negras y rostros pálidos . . .) (1992, 131)

The techniques of the impressionist painters (whose artistic innovations were a major influence in the development of modernist style) are evident in this and other sections of Darío's "En Chile"—especially the contrasts of a palette of light and dark tones. These, however, are not presented in the manner of the "colored prose or poetry" of previous periods. Instead, a full artistic range is employed, or, at the other end of the spectrum, a monochrome of blacks and whites as in "Charcoal" (Carbón):

> Suddenly I turned my eyes toward a dark corner. I saw a woman who was praying. *She was dressed in black* covered with a shawl; her highlighted face was severe, sublime, and in the background there was the vague dark outline of a confessional . . . the lights slowly dimmed, and with each moment the darkness of the background increased, and then dazzled; I seemed to see her face illuminated with a white, mysterious light . . .
>
> (De pronto, volví la vista cerca de mí, al lado de un ángulo de *sombra.* Había una mujer que oraba. *Vestía de negro,* envuelta en un manto, su rostro destacaba severo, sublime, teniendo por fondo la vaga oscuridad de un confesionario . . . las luces se iban extinguiendo, y a cada momento aumentaba lo osc-curo del fondo, y entonces, por un ofuscamiento, me parecía ver aquella faz iluminarse con una luz blanca y misteriosa . . .) (1992, 134)

And the narrator at that same moment draws the visionary moment to a close by focusing on the figure of the woman who, he confides, "would have made an ideal subject for a charcoal study" (habría sido un tema admirable para un estudio al carbón) (135).

Clearly an image-based program generated this and other Darío texts; the gaze, the passion for "painting with words," lies at the base of the Nica-raguan's ekphrastic discourse. If we turn to Darío's own explanation of the nature of his writing in his *History of My Books* (*Historia de mis libros*), a text in which he reflects upon the "novelties" of *Azul . . .* , we read that there was a conscious intent to supersede the clichés of Spanish Golden Age writing by taking inspiration from French authors, especially the symbolists in whose works he found new adjectival patterns, new syntactic molds, and a certain aristocratic verbal quality (1992, 195–196). But it is significant to point out that not only in the case of Darío, but also in that of other modernists of his generation, verbal experimentation was not simply a question of style pure and simple. Verbal innovations were connected to a need to fathom "the enigma of the universe's [contemporary] palpitations (200). In short, ekphrasis was not a hollow stylistic venture but was tied to the modernist's intense religious doubts, the generational angst and tedium that created a need to reorder and redefine the world, and in so doing, relocate the place of modern writers in the new socioeconomic structure of the early years of modernity. Darío, in writing about the genesis of "En Chile," characterized its miniatures as "chromatic sketches that had no antecedents in traditional Hispanic prose" (201).[16]

In his autobiographical comments on the genesis of "En Chile," Darío characterized his prose miniatures as "chromatic essays" (201). And the fact is that the brevity of these narrations, their mosaic quality, the agility of the prose constitute a reflection of a culture with accelerated movement, instability, and constant motion, a culture that produced emotional upsets and frustrations that assaulted and confused the modernists—all of which is apparent in their texts. They abound in stylistic experimentation, including the use of ekphrastic techniques by means of which they hoped to express a host of ideas and concerns without recourse to the outdated modes of writing of previous historical periods. Martí, who was endowed with a profound vision of his present and peered into the future, described all this in his essay "El carácter de la *Revista Venezolana*" (1881):

> we live in an age of incubation and renewal, in which having lost the old supports, we grope in search of new ones. . . . An Egyptian sky should not be painted with London fogs; nor the youthful verdure of our valleys with the pale green of Arcadia . . .

> (vivimos en una época de incubación y de rebrote, en que perdidos los antiguos quicios, andamos como a tientas en busca de los nuevos. . . . No se ha de pintar cielo de Egipto con brumas de Londres; ni el verdor juvenil de nuestros valles con aquel verde pálido de Arcadia . . .) (1963–1978, 7: 209, 211)

Krieger, writing from another vantage point, finds that the use of ekphrasis throughout history embraces a "desire to overcome the disadvantage of words and of the verbal art as mere arbitrary signs by forcing them to ape the natural signs and the natural-sign art that they cannot turn themselves into" (12). However, Darío and the majority of the Latin American modernists *were* successful in converting signs into temporal and spatial images through the use of plastic, sculptural, and even musical elements. The insistent use of ekphrasis by Darío and Martí reflected the cultural disconnects of their time and expressed the urgency felt by writers of their time to explore alternative universes through the medium of verbal power. The painted verbalizations of ekphrastic enunciations achieved a corporeal substantiality intended to fill the philosophical, social, and cultural voids of the waning decades of the nineteenth century, a void that in the following century was retextualized by vanguard writers and, in our day, by postmodernists.

2

PAINTED NARRATIONS

The Modernist Novel

Narrating modernity's unstable realities assumed a variety of forms in genres that included the novel, the short story, theater, *crónica*,[1] the prose poem, art criticism, and verse. The novel first appeared in Mexico in 1882 with the title *Por donde se sube al cielo* (The road to heaven), Manuel Gutiérrez Nájera's recently discovered, unfinished text,[2] which, though innovational—to a point—is still heavily influenced by romantic narrative techniques. Yet it set the tone for many of the modernist novels that followed.[3] By and large these novels—in spite of their individual originality and their heterogeneity with regard to style—are explorations of the inner self in a challenging, rapidly evolving new world.

Aníbal González, in his brief work on the modernist novel,[4] notes they deal with the role of the intellectual, the writer, or the artist in new social circumstances, a focus he identifies on the one hand with French origins, especially the Dreyfus affair, and, on the other as a product of the crisis created in Latin America by the Spanish American War (28). While these may be genuine attributions that serve to explain the rise of the modernist novel, in our view the genesis of these novels is more closely tied to the modernist writers' gaze at and reaction to the structural changes in Latin American society introduced by the advent of a new economic and social order and the resulting anguished sense of social, cultural, and political displacement the writers of the period experienced. In describing the shift in their social status—from the center to the periphery—Angel Rama explains that modernist writers lost the prominent cultural position many held in the old patriarchal order; briefly stated, they were thrown into the "marketplace" of early Latin American capitalism; they were faced with an unfamiliar set of social and cultural institutions. In an attempt to (re)define and (re)locate themselves, their gaze was no longer solely outward, as was the case of the major realistic and naturalistic novelists, but principally inward; and their inspiration was drawn from subjects both national and international, both contemporary and historical. By and large they tended to internalize the present and reinscribe the past in an effort to bring meaning to their contemporary confused and anomalous social universe. And although it may appear that the landscapes they painted were exotic or escapist, in fact, they were significant social, cultural, and even political introspections, *inscapes* that reflect an unstable, rapidly evolving social order and the ensuing struggle of writers and intellectuals to understand modernity's complexities and situate themselves within an uncharted social situation.

As early as 1881, Martí explained to his Venezuelan readers the need in Latin America for new forms of literary expression, linked their genesis to the contemporary social malaise, defended their appearance, and justified the use of nontraditional, experimental discourse. All of which, as was his custom, he expressed metaphorically:

> It is clear [he wrote] that we are passengers of a human ship, like all humanity, tossed around and toppled by huge waves; it is clear we were born in an age that scrutinizes, shouts, dislocates; neither the clamor, nor the advantages, nor the tasks of the embattled universe are unknown to us; it is also clear that having been born as humans, we suffer unusual distress, just like an eagle forced to live imprisoned in the tiny egg of a dove.

> (Cierto que, pasajeros de la nave humana, somos a par del resto de los hombres, revueltos y empujados por las grandes olas; cierto que, venido a la vida en época que escruta, vocea y disloca, ni los clamores, ni los provechos, ni las faenas del universo batallador nos son extrañas; cierto también que por nacer humanos, singulares dolores nos aquejan, como de águila forzada a vivir presa en un menguado huevecillo de paloma.)
> (1963–1973, 7: 210)

Further on, in this same essay—"El carácter de la *Revista Venezolana*"—he went on to say that faced with changing historical conditions, writers (by extension, artists and intellectuals) must speak with a different tongue given the nature of the changed environment in which they find themselves. Language, he indicated, must reflect the unfamiliar conditions of late nineteenth-century life: "You don't paint an Egyptian sky with a London fog" (No se ha de pintar cielo de Egipto con brumas de Londres) (7: 211), an apotegmic statement, previously cited, that summarized his theoretical stance with respect to the concept of "the new" in writing. And in both prose and poetry Martí painted. Cintio Vitier is one of the very few critics of Martí's work to note the persistent painterly style of his discourse.

> From his *El presidio político en Cuba* to his *Diario de campaña* Martí's writing is largely the work of a verbal painter—expressionist, impressionist, muralist, portraiture—without taking into account his anticipation of cinematographic techniques in many of his "Escenas norteamericanas" and in some of his *Versos sencillos* . . . (5)

Innovative narrative techniques and experimental language became the order of the day. The narratives generated by modernity, unlike the novels of realism and naturalism, were characterized by a conscious effort to produce a text highly artistic and polished in form; the novels of this period were shorter in length than traditional novels, frequently nonlinear in their plot development and in some cases had no plot at all, but were constructed with vignettes similar to those of Darío's "En Chile" examined in the preceding chapter. In short, modernist novels were experimental, "vanguard" narrations in which words acquired materiality and language was symbolic, pictorial, or musical. A host of new techniques were inspired by the reading of the texts of late nineteenth-century French writers (Baudelaire, Rimbaud, Mallarmé, Flaubert, Daudet, Zola, Gautier, Coppée, Verlaine, Catulle Mendès); other discursive elements were suggested by photographs of European paintings[5] and sculptures or were inspired by works of art viewed during visits to overseas museums. The novelists were influenced by impressionistic and expressionistic techniques in the works of French writers and painters or by the stylized chromatics of Japanese prints.[6] Imagination, even fantasy, dominated their narrative productions, which substantiated the generational disconnect with contemporary reality and gave rise to an inner countergaze. Emotions, strange passions, addictions, illicit liaisons, psychological disorders, imaginary nervous maladies became the stock in trade of the plots of many modernist novels. Modernity's reality, that is, the growth of a middle class in an age of industrialization and incipient capitalism in Latin America's major urban centers, resulted in an emphasis upon material acquisitions, opulent artistic works of art; imported exotic fabrics, gold jewelry, diamonds, rubies, opals, all made their way into the landscapes and inscapes of the works of these writers and contrasted with their counterdiscourses of spirituality and antimaterialism. The modernist writers were dazzled and attracted by the sensuous, aesthetic values of the products identified with the materialistic bourgeois culture they rejected, a culture that had ejected them from the central position they occupied in premodern society. Their imaginations were assaulted and injured by the complex, confusing ideological and philosophical amalgam of the Age of Modernity, the triumph of positivism and the subsequent dislocation of spiritual values espoused and cherished by modernist writers. Carlos Real de Azúa described the bewildering array of modernity's contradictory intellectual and artistic movements as a stage on the backdrop of which romantic, traditional, and bourgeois values were displayed; in the middle, positivism made its appearance, without entirely obliterating the values of the backdrop. And in the forefront, visibly placed, were the ideas espoused by a host of philosophers such as Nietzsche, Le Bon, Kropotkin, France, Tolstoy, Stirner, Schopenhauer, Ferri, Renan, Guyau, and Fouillée (15). Philosophies and ideas germinated (and also faded) at an accelerated pace late in the nineteenth century, a pattern that not only intensified the writers' and intellectuals' state of bewilderment, but also had the effect of amplifying their inward gaze as they attempted, frequently without success, to understand their new historical circumstances and sought solace from the social and cultural turmoil of the late nineteenth century. Given all these ideological, philosophic, aesthetic, and emotional factors it was not surprising that the modernist novels were characterized by individualism, by hybridity, and by what José Enrique Rodó termed the inharmonic variety of the times, the sign of an age of cultural transition.[7] Or as Martí put it, an age of readjustments and reconfigurations.[8] In their works the modernists sought to engage spiritual values and employ the fullest range of the senses.

The brevity of these narrations to which we've alluded was more than likely a reflection of the staccato, agitated rhythm of modernity, a pace Martí characterized as a "turbulent stream" (19: 114). Foreshadowing Marinetti's futuristic aesthetic of restlessness and constant movement, the Latin American modernists distilled and compressed the velocity of life in their novels and presented its bits and pieces in minimalistic narrations such as Efrén Rebolledo's *Salamandra* (1919)—a brief narration (seventy-two pages) whose action unfolds in Mexico during the last years of the nineteenth century. Dandy, decadent, and byzantine, the novel's norms and its prose are carefully crafted—sculpted—to achieve the maximum aesthetic effects of a narration in which the dissolute life of the wealthy bourgeoisie is presented via the machinations of Elena, a cold, calculating socialite intent on destroying her male admirer (shades of Baudelaire). The descriptions of Elena's luxurious home constitute canvases of color, line, and texture (1968, 25); a visit to a gallery evokes the chromatics of a painting with its emphasis on blues and violets reminiscent of the Barbizon painters with their blurred forms and limited range of color: "Although the lines [of the canvases] were rigid, the colors were weak, with blue and violet predominating" (Aunque la línea [of the canvases] era firme, era débil el colorido, con predominio del azul y del violeta) (47).

Modernity's varied novelistic practices can best be exemplified in the narrations of two major writers of the period: in José Martí's *Lucía Jerez* and José Asunción Silva's *De sobremesa*. Both writers are cognizant of the outer world, both explore the hidden recesses of human emotions, the wellsprings of artistic creativity, and both are attracted to the very objects of beauty and wealth of the materialistic culture they abjure. And, finally, both, in connection with the painting of modernism, construct painterly narrations, blend language and plasticity in an aesthetic gaze that endeavors to define and question the realities of modernity's factious discourses.

LUCÍA JEREZ

Martí's novel was originally entitled *Amistad funesta* (Fatal friendship). It was not a work he intended to write. A friend of his, Adelaida Baralt, received a commission to write a novel for *El Latino-Americano*, a New York periodical of the late nineteenth century. Its editor specified that the novel was to have "lots of romance, a death, lots of young girls, no illicit affairs, nothing that would violate family values or offend priests—and the subject matter was to be Latin American" (Martí 1963–1973, 18: 192). It's difficult to imagine how a major novel could be composed given the confining strictures of the editor. Be that as it may, Adelaida accepted the commission but quickly discovered she was incapable of writing the novel and asked Martí to write it in her place. Martí, who at the time was not particularly well disposed toward the novel as a literary genre, accepted the challenge, and legend has it he finished the commissioned narrative in seven days if we give credence to his "biblical" confession with respect to its genesis. Later in life, given the popularity and the political storm Helen Hunt Jackson's novel *Ramona* created, he revised his opinion of the novel, reconsidered its value as a social instrument, translated both *Ramona* and Hugh Conway's[9] *Called Back* (1883; *Misterio*), and in his notebooks developed the elements of a novel he planned on writing. But in 1885, faced with the task of creating the serialized chapters of *Amistad funesta*, he expressed serious doubts about the success of his undertaking. And three years prior to publishing his novel in a letter to his sister, Amelia, he wrote: "Do not be taken in, my beautiful Amelia, by the endearments described in crass novels, and hardly a novel is not vulgar, written as they are by those incapable of writing more elevated works . . ." (1993, 1: 224).[10] But in spite of his misgivings about the quality of the novels of his time, and without realizing fully the importance of his undertaking, with the writing of *Amistad funesta* he produced one of the most significant and original early Latin American narratives that belong to a corpus that chronicles the imbalances of the chaotic process of nineteenth-century Latin American modernization.[11] The reason we use the adverb *fully* in describing Martí's disdain for his narrative is that corrections to the clippings of his published *El Latino-Americano* text left in Martí's office on Front Street in New York City were discovered at an unspecified later date by his colleague and secretary, Gonzalo de Quesada y Aróstegui. And when the latter asked Martí about them, Martí waved them aside, remarking they were merely a product of struggles and sad moments belonging to the past. However, history shows us the Cuban did not dismiss them entirely, for he instructed Quesada to keep them for a later date (18: 187), and, the fact is, he ended up planning a second printing of the novel with the textual modifications Quesada discovered, an introduction (unfinished), and the revised title by which the novel is known today: *Lucía Jerez*.

Structurally, the novel is composed of three chapters and is shorter in length when compared to the novels of the realists and naturalists. However, the discourse and aesthetics are diametrically opposite. Martí's novel, for example, from the very first paragraph reveals the hand of a painter of words. And, in fact, many are the paragraphs that, if extracted from the narrative's plot development, might well stand alone as prose poems transposed and projected on a canvas. For example, the opening of chapter 1 reads as follows:

> A luxuriant magnolia, trimmed too fastidiously by the local gardener, shaded Lucía Jerez's visitors that Sunday morning. Under a clear sky in the patio of the lovely house, the magnolia's huge white flowers, fully open on its branches of delicate, sharp leaves, did not seem to be tree flowers, but flowers belonging to that day!, huge, immaculate flowers one conjures up when one loves too much.

(Una frondosa magnolia, podada por el jardinero de la casa
con manos demasiado académicas, cubría aquel domingo por la
mañana con su sombra a los familiares de la casa de Lucía Jerez.
Las grandes flores blancas de la magnolia, plenamente abiertas
en sus ramas de hojas delgadas y puntiagudas, no parecían, bajo
aquel cielo claro y en el patio de aquella casa amable, las flores
del árbol, sino las del día, ¡esas flores inmensas e inmaculadas,
que se imaginan cuando se ama mucho!) (1)

The painterly vision throughout the novel is interspersed with moral
observations that we consider related to and emanating from the conflicted
psyche of modernist writers. The observations, in Martí's case, are socially or ethically based constructions created with metaphors of light and
dark:

The human soul has a great need of whiteness. When whiteness
darkens, misfortune rushes in. The practice and consciousness
of virtue, the possession of the best qualities, the arrogance of
the most noble sacrifices, are insufficient to soothe the soul for
a single blunder.

(El alma humana tiene una gran necesidad de blancura. Desde
que lo blanco se oscurece, la desdicha empieza. La práctica y
conciencia de todas las virtudes, la posesión de las mejores
cualidades, la arrogancia de los más nobles sacrificios, no bas-
tan a consolar el alma de un solo extravío.) (1)

Note how Martí moves from the general to the specific—from the "human
soul" (general) the field of his view is directed toward the individual
("soul," "single blunder"), a movement sustained at the beginning of the
following paragraph in which he continues to "color" his canvas-like discourse with splashes of bright light and patches of blue green and white in
the style of the late nineteenth-century impressionist painters:

The three friends in their wicker rocking chairs, adorned with
bows of ribbon, were lovely to see on that Sunday, under the
bright sun, the blue light, between the columns of marble, the
elegant magnolia, between the green branches with the huge
white flowers . . .

> (Eran hermosas de ver, en aquel domingo, en el cielo fulgente,
> la luz azul, y por entre los corredores de columnas de mármol,
> la magnolia elegante, entre las ramas verdes, las grandes flores
> blancas y en sus mecedoras de mimbre, adornadas con lazos de
> cinta . . .) (1)

Lucía Jerez, as stated at the outset, is an experimental novel much in advance of narrative innovations that follow, or what Freedman (25) has termed the "lyrical novel":

> In conventional narratives [writes Freedman], the outer world
> is the thing. It is placed beyond both writer and reader, inter-
> posing between them and the theme. In the lyrical mode, such
> a world is conceived, not as a universe in which men display
> their action, but as a poet's vision fashioned as a design. The
> world is reduced to a *lyrical point of view*, the equivalent of the
> poet's "I." (8; emphasis mine)

These novels, and Martí's in particular, are vanguard compositions not merely in the use of color and painterly techniques but in the exploitation of motion, symbolically applied much before Marinetti's "futuristic" treatises that exalted the beauty of speed (1909, 1912)[12] in life, art, and literature. In this regard, it's significant to point out that among the "futuristic" elements of Martí's narration is the use of movement to plumb the depths of the emotional fiber of his characters. As if he were assembling a motorized, programmed contemporary installation piece, the narrator's eye catches the symbolic movements of the women gathered on Lucía Jerez's patio on a Sunday afternoon:

> Ana's rocking chair was still, and on her pale lips there was a
> constant smile: her eyes contemplated the violets in her lap as
> if they should always be there. Adela, with difficulty remained
> seated in her rocker, which sometimes was near Ana, other
> times near Lucía, and most of the time empty. Lucía's chair
> more frequently was positioned forward, rather than back, and
> changed its position suddenly, as if obeying an energetic, con-
> tained movement of its occupant.

> (La mecedora de Ana no se movía, tal como apenas en sus
> labios pálidos la afable sonrisa: se buscaban con los ojos las vio-

letas en su falda, como si siempre debiera estar llena de ellas. Adela no sin esfuerzo se mantenía en su mecedora, que unas veces estaba cerca de Ana, otras de Lucía, y vacía las más. La mecedora de Lucía, más echada hacia adelante que hacia atrás, cambiaba de súbito de posición, como obediente a un gesto enérgico y contenido de su dueña.) (3)

The entire passage exhibits a variety of movements or their absence. Speed or rapid acceleration serves as a metaphor to characterize the inner emotional or psychological ticks of each of the women without the lengthy descriptive verbiage of the realists. Martí constantly "speaks" in metaphors, or in colors (e.g., violet = symbol of pain and death), or uses movement (modernized life reflected in the individual psyche) to advance the development of his narration. Action becomes symbolic when, for example, Lucía, who suffers from an abnormal inclination toward jealousy, in a fit of traumatic emotion resulting from what she perceives to be her fiancé's excessive attention to Ana's art, instead of verbalizing her indignation, literally strangles her handkerchief:

> . . . what right did Juan have to forget Lucía [observes the narrator] while standing next to her by paying so much attention to Ana's eccentricities? . . . and with nervous gestures she rolled her delicate batiste and lace handkerchief around her index finger. And she rolled it so much and unrolled it with such violence, passing it rapidly from one hand to the other, that the handkerchief took on the appearance of a reptile, one of those white snakes found in coastal Yucatan. . . . Lucía stood up with a movement that seemed a leap; and Juan picked up her torn handkerchief from the ground in order to return it to her.

> (. . . ¿qué derecho tenía Juan a olvidarse tanto de Lucía, y estando a su lado, poner tanta atención a las rarezas de Ana? . . . [y] enrollaba nerviosamente en el dedo índice de la mano izquierda un finísimo pañuelo de batista y encaje. Y lo enrolló tanto y tanto, y lo desenrollaba con tal violencia, que, yendo rápidamente de una mano a la otra, el lindo pañuelo parecía una víbora, una de esas víboras blancas que se ven en la costa yucateca. . . . Se puso de pie Lucía con un movimiento que pareció un salto; y Juan alzó del suelo, para devolvérselo, el pañuelo roto.) (18–19)

The "eccentricities" of Lucía's friend, Ana, are paintings that the narrator tells us have a musical quality ("cuadritos que parecen música"), full of light. Their unusual qualities suggest their characterization as handpainted photos, and they are, without question, the product of the unconscious liberation of the mind via dreams; in short they are a precursor of surrealist painting. Her latest canvas (characterized by the narrator as "strange") and described ekphrastically with symbolic enunciations, shows a handsome young man wearing an elegant gray suit who looks at his hands in amazement. He has just crushed a lily that has fallen at his feet, and his hands are covered in blood (16). The symbolism is blatantly moral; Ana herself says, following the narrator's pictorial transposition[13] and addressing her remarks to Pedro, that she hoped her painting would be successful among men who destroy or sully lilies (e.g., virginity) (16). She then goes on to describe a second painting, equally surrealist in nature but still in the planning stage:

> I'm going to paint a monster seated atop a hill. I'll paint a full moon whose rays will fall over the back of the monster and allow me to simulate with highlighted bands of light the most famous Parisian buildings. And while the moon caresses the [monster's] backside and we see by contrast the outline of its luminous figure, all the darkness of its body, the monster, with the head of a woman will be devouring roses. And in the corner emaciated and disheveled young women who are fleeing with their dresses torn raising their hands up to the sky.

> (Sobre una colina voy a pintar un monstruo sentado. Pondré la luna en cenit, para que caiga de lleno sobre el lomo del monstruo, y me permita simular con líneas de luz en las partes salientes los edificios de París más famosos. Y mientras la luna le acaricia el lomo, y se ve por el contraste del perfil luminoso toda la negrura de su cuerpo, el monstruo, con cabeza de mujer, estará devorando rosas. Allá por un rincón se verán jóvenes flacas y desmelenadas que huyen con las túnicas rotas, levantando las manos al cielo.) (17)

The planned canvas has the light and broad strokes of the late nineteenth-century impressionists with the vibrant symbolism of the expressionists. In fact, her symbolic canvases that she and her friends viewed as strange and unusual foreshadowed expressionistic and/or surrealist painterly techniques in sync with Martí's frequently metaphorical discourse. At times, the narrator of *Lucía Jerez* conjoined visual and musical effects reminiscent of Baudelaire's search for synaesthetic juxtapositions, producing prose poems such as the description of the emotionally exhausted Hungarian pianist Keleffy's concert in Havana related in chapter 3, the conclusion of which transforms musical tones into a pale canvas:

> He traveled because he was consumed by eagles who were devouring his body. . . . He traveled because he married a woman whom he thought he loved, but found her to be a silent goblet . . . until a friend took him by the arm and said "Cure yourself." . . . Keleffy [that night] performed some of his delicate compositions on the ebony piano that under his hands at times seemed a psaltery, a flute at times, at times an organ, not those [compositions] in which it might be said the ocean swelled like mountains and fell shattered like crystal shards, or a man wrestled a bull, and split the crown of its head, and bent its legs and threw it on the ground, but the other delicate fantasies, *which if they had color, would have been pale, and if visible, would have been a landscape at dusk.*

> (Viajaba porque estaba lleno de águilas, que le comían el cuerpo . . . Viajaba porque casó con una mujer a quien creyó amar, y la halló luego como una copa sorda . . . hasta que lo tomó un amigo leal del brazo, y le dijo "Cúrate." . . . Keleffy [esa noche] tocó en el piano de madera negra, que bajo sus manos parecía a veces salterio, flauta a veces, y a veces órgano, algunas de sus delicadas composiciones, no aquellas en que se hubiera dicho que el mar subía en montes y caía roto en cristales, o que braceaba un hombre con un toro, y le hendía el testuz, y le doblaba las piernas y lo echaba por tierra, sino aquellas otras flexibles fantasías que, a tener color, hubieran sido pálidas, y a ser cosas visibles, hubiesen parecido un paisaje de crepúsculo.) (36–38; emphasis mine)

The final words suggest an impressionist canvas, especially the pallid tones of a twilight luminescence.

Quite different in tone and quality is the sybaritic description of one of the rooms of Lucía's home. The objects in it are those that belong to the Parnassian aesthetic of mid-nineteenth-century France with its emphasis upon line, color, marble, gold, silver, and the broad spectrum of objects of bourgeois wealth that modernity ushered in. The Latin American modernist writers, both in prose and poetry, were fascinated with what the French Parnassians termed the *noble* (i.e., valued) *objects of luxury*, which they folded into their discourse and which Martí included in his novel. Colors, chiaroscuro, onyx, bronze, the artistry of the moment and that of the ancient past, are blended in a sensuous and elegant description of the affluent décor of Lucía's home:

> The entrance hall was elegant and small as it had to be in order to be elegant. From braided crystal tulips that hung as a branch suspended from the ceiling by a tube hidden among bronzed tulip leaves the soft orange light, emanating from the incandescent electric fixture, fell upon an onyx table. . . . The delicately colored mosaic floor reminiscent of Pompeian vestibules had the embedded inscription "Salve." . . . It's always important to have before one's eyes beautiful objects . . . decorating the walls and heightening with color that brightens and dissipates the shadows of the corners.

> (La antesala era linda y pequeña, como que se tiene que ser pequeño para ser lindo. De unos tulipanes de cristal trenzado, suspendidos en un ramo del techo por un tubo oculto entre hojas de tulipán simuladas en bronce, caía sobre la mesa de ónix la claridad anaranjada y suave de la lámpara de luz elétrica incandescente. . . . El pavimento de mosaico de colores tenues que, como el de los atrios de Pompeya, tenía la inscripción "Salve." . . . Conviene tener siempre delante de los ojos . . . ornando las paredes, animados los rincones donde se refugia la sombra, objetos bellos, que la coloreen y la disipen.)
> (11)

The vision Martí develops in his novel is that of a fractured world. At the beginning of the novel's fourth serialization, the narrator alludes to a broken glass, to a building in ruins, to a fallen palm—metaphors of a ravaged reality. The metaphoric enunciations are subsequently explicated as the narrator reveals the ideological base of his work:

> These are unhinged times and with the crumbling of the previous social barriers and their educational refinements, a new

and vast class of intelligent aristocrats has been created, with all the needs of comportment and taste of the wealthy that derive from their new status, but without enough time having passed as yet, given the rapidity of the shift, for the change in the organization and distribution of fortunes to produce a quick alteration in social relationships as a result of the political liberties and the popularization of knowledge . . . wealth is the stomach of happiness. Husbands, lovers, those who still have to live and hope to prosper: organize your budgets!

(Estos tiempos nuestros están desquiciados, y con el derrumbe de las antiguas vallas sociales y las finezas de la educación, ha venido a crearse una nueva y vastísima clase de aristócratas de la inteligencia, con todas las necesidades de parecer y gustos ricos que de ella vienen, sin que haya habido tiempo aún, en lo rápido del vuelo, para que el cambio en la organización y repartimiento de las fortunas corresponda a la brusca alteración en las relaciones socialees, producidas por las libertades políticas y la vulgarización de los conocimientos . . . la hacienda es el estómago de la felicidad. Maridos, amantes, personas que aún tenéis que vivir y anheláis prosperar: ¡organizad bien vuestra hacienda! (90–91)

In this "universal instability" (desequilibrio universal) (91), Lucía and Juan's symbolic and dramatic existence is narrated with color, line, contrasts of light and dark, and musical tones. It is Lucía who creates the tension and violence of the work—a violence connected to the process of modernization whose effects were felt in the culture, education, economy, private life, and social relationships of the period.

DE SOBREMESA

As was the case of Martí and Gutiérrez Nájera, José Asunción Silva produced a single novel. But his novel, *De sobremesa*, has come down to us in a revised form. Max Henríquez Ureña, a historian of Latin American modernism, tells us that it was originally written in Caracas where Silva served as a diplomat during 1894. But on his return home to Bogotá, his ship, *L'Amérique*, foundered and his trunk with the manuscripts of six short novels (*Cuentos negros*), a book of sonnets (*Poemas de la carne*), and the original *De sobremesa* sank to the bottom of the sea.[14] Of all the lost manuscripts only one, that of the novel, was rewritten and published posthumously in 1925, twenty-nine years after Silva's death.

In his 1996 edition of Silva's novel, Gabriel García Márquez writes that the gaze of the novelist is that of a cineast: "The concept of space [he notes], the expressive use of light, the plasticity of the décor of the salon belonging to the wealthy in the waning years of the nineteenth century in Paris, the strategy used to present the main characters are cinematic techniques" (14; translation mine). In this, as in the use of some of the painterly techniques we've examined earlier, there is an anticipation of artistic innovations: that is, as we suggested at the very beginning of our study, a capturing of reality through the focused lens of a camera. Once again, it is García Márquez who points out a previously unnoticed technique of Silva's narration—his clairvoyance with respect to the use of cinematic techniques, including zooming and the use of color. It's significant to note that the Colombian modernist died only four months after the Lumière brothers' first film venture in France and before Marie-Georges-Jean Méliès's use of special film effects in 1896 (14), effects that transformed reality and earned him the title of "cinemagician." In Silva's case, his "camera's eye" focuses and records the light, colors, textures, and the physical appearance of the characters seated in the protagonist José Fernández's salon at the beginning of his novel, a space to which he returns in cyclical fashion at the conclusion of the novel, which ends with the suspended reading of José Fernández's diary. Chromatics, contrasts of light and dark, exotic objects of luxury and expensive taste meet the eye of the reader at the outset of the novel, in a painterly transposition much as the spectator would see the scene in a film, or alternatively, in literary terms, as a cinematic ekphrasis:

> A lethargic crimson semi-darkness enveloped the room. The delicate smoke of the Oriental cigarettes fluttered in subtle spirals in the circle of light dimmed by the lampshade's antique lace. The white of the fragile China cups contrasted with the blood red color of the velvet tablecloth, and at the bottom of the cut crystal decanter with its transparent Dantzig liquor, the atoms of gold danced with a luminosity reminiscent of a fairy tale.

> (Adormecíase en él la semioscuridad carmesí del aposento. El humo tenue de los cigarillos de Oriente ondeaba en sutiles espirales en el círculo de luz de la lámpara atenuada por la pantalla de encajes antiguos. Blanqueaban las frágiles tazas de

china sobre el terciopelo color de sangre de la carpeta, y en el fondo del frasco de cristal tallado, entre la transparencia del aguardiente de Dantzig, los átamos de oro se agitaban luminosos bailando una ronda, fantástica como un cuento de hadas.) (228)

Silva's novel is filled with intense "visions," especially those of Helena, whom José Fernández claimed to have seen briefly one night in the restaurant of a Geneva hotel. Helena, envisioned and sublimated by Fernández, becomes the mainspring and motivating core of his existence. He searches worldwide for the elusive Helena "seen" by him on that single night, who has been transformed by him into the passion at the center of his life. But after months of febrile, futile imaginings, agonizing visions, and worldwide searches, when he finally consults a "psychophysician," Doctor Rivington, the doctor tries to convince him that Helena was not actually seen by Fernández in Geneva. Instead, he finds, she is the product of the protagonist's imagination, which has converted the subject of a Pre-Raphaelite painting, seen in a London exhibition years ago, into the living vision he claims to have seen in Geneva. And, by the strangest of circumstances, Dr. Rivington has that very painting in one of the rooms of his medical suite.

After viewing the doctor's canvas, and following a prolonged fever connected to what has the appearance of a nervous breakdown, one day a copy of the painting housed in the doctor's office arrives in Fernández's apartment. But prior to the receipt of the copy, Fernández had immersed himself in a study of the Pre-Raphaelite school of painting, including a major figure of the movement, and the reasons, he claimed, determined the rise of the Brotherhood in the art world. He studied details of the life of Beato Angélico de Fiésole, read the letters of Rossetti and Holman Hunt, the verses of William Morris and Swinburne, and admired the canvases of Rossetti and Sir Edward Burne-Jones. Totally steeped in the literature and the art of the Pre-Raphaelites, Fernández's immersion allowed him to say that the painting of Helena was "a perfect specimen of the techniques of the Pre-Raphaelite Brotherhood; its noble figure [had] practically no movement, turned to one side but looking straight ahead . . ." (un perfecto espécimen de los procedimientos de la cofradía prerrafaelista; casi nulo el movimiento de la figura noble colocada de tres cuartos y mirando de frente . . .) (162). The painting so described was what, among the artists of the period, would be considered a *translation* of the copy,[15] and is viewed and admired by the enthralled Fernández:

> . . . the line and color of the marvelous tiny bare feet visible
> beneath the complex byzantine trim of the white tunic and
> the long, thin hands suspended from the wrists in the style of
> Parmagiano [*sic*],[16] . . . clasped to hold a bouquet of lilies . . .
>
> (. . . maravillosos por el dibujo y por el color los piesecitos des-
> nudos que asoman bajo el oro de la complicada orla bizantina
> que borda la túnica blanca y las manos afiladas y largas . . . al
> modo de las figuras del Parmagiano, se juntan para sostener el
> manojo de lirios . . .) (162–163)

And the narration goes on to detail all of the canvas's features, its lines
and color, down to the bottom of the painting on which appear in gilt the
words: MANIBUS DATE LILIA PLENIS.[17]

A second painting hangs in the same room—a portrait of José Fernández's grandmother painted by James MacNeil [*sic*] Whistler,[18] an innovative artist who conceived of his canvases as "harmonies," in the tradition
of modernism's hybridities.

The narration, pages ahead (184–188), focuses on alternative visual perceptions: those inspired by the Parnassians' fascination with precious stones. The diary contains a narration different from the entry that
describes the two paintings the protagonist has hung in a special room decorated and maintained as a spiritual sanctuary in his Paris home. From the
cloistered space of his dwelling we are transported to an urban alternative
interior location, that of Bassot's elegant jewelry shop, where Fernández
stands, entranced by the sensuous beauty of the precious stones displayed
in the store's cases, all of which pass before the eye of the narrator who
personifies them and bedazzles them before the eyes of the reader with the
sensuous detail of a painter:

> Oh, sparkling gems, splendid, invulnerable, vivid stones, you
> who lay dormant for entire centuries in the bowels of the
> planet, the eye's delight, symbol and compendium of human
> wealth! The diamonds sparkle and shine like drops of light;
> they are like fragments of the tropical sky on nights constel-
> lated with dark sapphires; you, ruby, you burn like crystallized
> blood; the emeralds display the diaphanous greens of my coun-
> try in their luminous crystals . . .
>
> (¡Oh, piedras rutilantes, espléndidas e invulnerables, vívi-
> das gemas que dormisteis por siglos enteros en las entrañas

del planeta, delicia del ojo, símbolo y resumen de las riquezas humanas!. Los diamantes se irisan y brillan como gotas de luz; semejan pedazos del cielo del trópico en las noches consteladas los oscuros zafiro; tú, rubí, ardes como una cristalización de sangre; las esmeraldas ostentan en sus cristales luminosos los verdes diáfanos de los bosques de mi tierra . . .) (184–185)

Silva's eye as it moves from stone to stone creates a chromatic collage of irradiating flashes of light; in short we "read" a canvas of resplendent color in a rhapsodic prose poem that in its final lines attributes a symbolic value to each of the stones (185).

Not all of the painterly discourses of this novel are inspired by European—principally French and English—models. The eye of the novelist encompasses a much broader artistic universe, one that includes the Far East, much admired and incorporated in many ways in the modern literary texts of Silva's contemporaries. The artistic creations and the material products of China and Japan, viewed as exotica, fill the pages of this novel, from its beginning to its conclusion. Directing his voice to the workers of the world who spend their life doubled up, brutalized by hard work and an impoverished diet (178, 181) and to readers who now are asking for works that entertain less and instead make them think and see the mystery hidden in each particle of the "grand universe," the narrator asks,

> Do you, spirit who questions the future and sees the old religions crumble, still doubt there is a renaissance of idealism and neo-mysticism . . . from the dark bedrock of the Orient, land of the gods, Buddhism and magic are reconquering the West . . .

> (¿Dudas todavía del renacimiento idealista y del neo-misticismo, espíritu que inquieres el futuro y ves desplomarse las Viejas religiones? . . . Mira: del oscuro fondo del Oriente, patria de los dioses, vuelven el budismo y la magia a reconquistar el mundo occidental.) (181–182)

Elsewhere the narrator refers to the "subtleties of Japanese art" (93); to Japanese silk (70); to the fragile Chinese teacups (71); or the opiated tobacco of the Orient (31).

This novel, written in the form of a diary, is at times a diary within a diary, for at one point it is composed of portions of Marie Bashkirtseff's diary,[19] including her passionate need to paint, which Silva retextualizes and describes in the form of a transposed canvas: "I have to fight [the narrator tells us the agonizing Russian writes] I have to live. I must paint the Holy Women guarding the sepulcher" (¡Hay que luchar, hay que vivir! Hay que pintar las Santas Mujeres guardando el sepulcro) (53). There then follows a lengthy visual description of a canvas in which Mary's somber silhouette is foregrounded with her tears and her mood of desperation. The scene, we read via Silva, which Marie Bashkirtseff is moved to paint, is followed with the refrain: "I must paint; I must paint" (54). And it would not be exaggerating to say that Silva, like Bashkirtseff, is also moved to paint, to paint a modern narrative of mystic spirituality, lust, and degeneration. But, in addition, his, like so many other narratives of the late nineteenth century, is also a work that proposes change in the form of modernization, with a clarion call for industrialization and/or economic progress. Aesthetics, spirituality, and art are thus intertwined in this and other modernist novels in which hybridity is a reflection of the conflicted cultural, social, and political aspirations of the early Age of Modernity. Their hybridity, contradictions, and even their ambiguity suggest a tacit process of undoing the order of late nineteenth- and early twentieth-century bourgeois society.

3

FROM PAINTING TO LITERARY TEXT

POLLICE VERSO: LIFE IS A BROAD ARENA

The discussion and analysis in this chapter is based upon three textual elements: 1) A painting by the French artist Jean-León Gérome entitled *Pollice verso*; 2) a Martí essay in which the Cuban modernist reviews the works seen by him in a New York gallery, including the canvas *Pollice verso*; and 3) a poem (*Versos libres*)[1] the Cuban wrote afterward, inspired by the French painting, elements of which he transposes in some of the verses of his lengthy poem but the message of which he alters in order to express a liberation project that is diametrically opposed to the canvas's message.

Martí's liberation project is enunciated in a counterhegemonic discourse that questions the marketplace laws of the incipient process of capitalism and its political and economic forces. His is a discourse that also questions the bases of modernity, including its aesthetic and artistic values. In their place he proposes a reformulation of the idea of the new, of what is culturally valid for Latin America in a period of transition and redefinition—the period of the last two decades of the nineteenth century. The normative principles of his ideology are illustrated paradigmatically in necrological notes on the French sculptor François Dumaine in an essay in which he observes that "art will save the Latin countries, the book, the Anglo-Saxon peoples; the former's confidence is built upon a religion that rests on beauty that they trust as aiding virtue, improving weak spirits and a fertile source of grandeur" (los pueblos latinos se salvan por el arte, como los sajones se salvan por el libro, y en la religion de la belleza, fían, como auxiliadora de toda virtud, mejoradora de espíritus débiles, y creadora fecunda de grandezas) (1963–1973, 6: 412).[2] And at the end of this note (which belongs to Martí's Mexican period) he added, "national liberty stimulated the belief system of the modern spirit as well as all the forms of the new life [of our time]" (la libertad nacional [es la] animadora de todas las creencias del moderno espíritu y todas las formas de la nueva vida) (6: 413). Beauty and modernity, he was convinced, were identified with a revolutionary, emancipatory, national art. For him, the nexus between art and poetry generated new articulations, a process by which contemporary texts, as well as those belonging to the past, created new signs, and the original text—as exemplified by "Pollice verso"—thus becomes an intertext in which signs—those of the past, for example—are transformed and speak to the present as well as to the future.

In order to examine this complex array of texts and values, we take as our point of departure with regard to aesthetics and the notions of nationhood and liberty, Martí's principle: "I must see before I begin to write" (Necesito ver antes lo que he de escribir) (1935–1953, 52: 128), a visionary precept expressed in one of the many scattered notes he penned in his workbooks. This principle, one of his seminal innovative ideas, is one that defines the modern subject's appropriation of the techniques of other arts and incorporates them in "transpositions," transtextualizations, or intertexts by means of which the techniques of painting, for example, are transferred to those of literature with the hope of broadening the limits of verbal expression and encompassing and (re)organizing reality and the values of modernity's culture.

"Pollice verso" (*Versos libres*), which contains the line "Life is a broad arena," is one of many Martí texts in which a painting becomes a poem.[3] It was written after Martí viewed one of Jean-Léon Gérome's paintings with the same title in New York's Stewart Gallery. On this and other canvases of the French painter Martí devoted part of an essay he sent to the *Nación* of Buenos Aires in 1887. In it he mentions the painting twice, but it's apparent that Gérome was not among Martí's favorite painters because his comments are not comparable to the praise he heaps upon Spanish painters such as Fortuny or Zamacois. He observes, for example, that "the 'Race' and 'Pollice verso' by Gérome are more celebrated *than they should be*, because in them the interest of the theme is not at the same level as the intent and skill of the execution" ("La Carrera" y el "Pollice verso" de Gérome [son] más celebres que dignos de serlo, puesto que en ellos no iguala al *interés del tema* la decisión y la sabiduría de la pintura" (1963–1978, 19: 316; emphasis mine). Why then, we might well ask, does he devote a poem to *Pollice verso* if the painting doesn't excite him? Clearly he was attracted by the theme as he himself confessed, and, moreover, it is more than likely that in the "varnished" Gérome canvas he identified with some "deep symbols" such as those that enthused him in Mariano Fortuny's paintings, especially the canvas entitled *The Snake Charmer*, which he described in the following way:

> [It] reveals that strange power of a genius capable of creating deep symbols in an involuntary way from the nature that inspired the work. . . . The chair is like [the Arab of the painting], elegant and fine: it represents liberty; raw life, in a cloud of hashish; the race inflames the heart; . . . the friend in danger and the pillow in death.

> ("El encantador" revela ese extraño poder del genio para crear involuntariamente *símbolos profundos* de la naturaleza que lo inspira. . . . La silla es como él [el árabe del cuadro], elegante y fina: *ella es la libertad*; la vida fiera, en una nube de haschisch; la carrera que inflama el corazón; el turbión de arena en que resplandece la espingarda; la amiga en el peligro y la almohada en la muerte.) (1963–1973, 19: 318; emphasis mine)

It is more than evident that in Fortuny's art Martí discovered the elements he valued in aesthetic relationships—whether plastic or literary—that is, conflict, dynamism, liberty, concepts that surface in his criticism of Fortuny and in his poem "Pollice verso," in which poetic art is expressed within a construct of liberty tied to the creation of nationhood and in which ethical and aesthetic elements are fused in a harmonious and rhythmic dynamic.

As an art critic Martí grasped in Gérome's painting the sense of the painter's inspiration.[4] His commentary about the "interest of the theme" prefigures later criticism, which notes that "his strange art records the conflicted emergence of an equally strange new world" (Knight). Similarly, Martí perceived parallelisms in *his* "Pollice verso" between the events of Roman life and modern life as well as in connection with the Cuban nation. His comments on historical cycles joined to a personal love for things Roman touched his soul, perhaps without his realizing to what extent, as he viewed Gérome's work. History, translated into a personal experience of his infancy, surely played a decisive role in appreciating Gérome's canvas in spite of what he considered the French painter's much-too-academic style. Recalling the days of his infancy and his early inclination toward the idea of painting in verse, he wrote:

Who would have told me that while still a child, and a daring
one, that I attempted to *paint in verse* the imposing energy of
Regulus? And I remember that in my childhood . . . flights of
fantasy I imagined that sometimes I had a Roman soul.

(¿Quién me dijo a mí, cuando niño aún, y por serlo, osado,
intenté *pintar en verso* la energía imponente de Régulo? Y recuerdo que en mis atrevimientos infantiles, volaba hasta él mi
espíritu, y llegaba en el vuelo a imaginarse que *tenía de vez en
cuando alma romana*) (1963–1973, 19: 416; emphasis mine)

Our argument, therefore, in relation to the visual elements in Martí's
creative process, and, returning to his sentence "I must see before I begin
to write," is that his childhood memories constitute a retextualized past
in his art, a past that takes conscious or unconscious form as he views
Gérome's work in the Stewart Gallery. This generative process and his
retextualization of the past is more than supposition in the light of the
following incomplete observation of the Cuban poet: "We have sleeping
images in our soul. *Let us paint life*—not accept it as it is" (Tenemos en
el alma dormidas las imágenes. *Pintar la vida*—no conformarse con ella)
(1963–1978, 19: 418; emphasis mine). In other words, life for him was not
limited to material or visible circumstances, nor to a faithful reproduction
of a given reality;[5] the modern artist visualizes subjectively and reinscribes
reality. On another occasion he stated that an individual's history "is a
brief summary of historical life"; one more reason to explain why Gérome's
"Pollice verso" inspired him, for in the Roman history of the canvas he
discovered a triple significance: the memory of his past in the penitentiary,
a commentary on the present, and a warning for an oppressed and suffering
people—the people of colonial Cuba.

In examining the transpositional process of Martí's poem, the lexicon
of the *battle*—*gladiator, combat, shield, arena*—constitutes a major inspira-
tional element. It becomes a means by which the poet revives himself, a
way in which he saves himself as he contemplates the works of Fortuny,
Jean-Louis-Ernest Meissonier, and Gérome, among others. Viewing and
thinking of the paintings he sees in the gallery, he tries, as he writes in his
essay, to rekindle his spirit:

Whoever suffers from the sour life of this sordid community[6]
cannot fail to see that these delightful creations strike a hungry
soul as a shower of luminous and winged fruits. They constitute
a collection of sobering paintings, they show the exercise of

spiritual brushwork, battles amid whose din this century was ushered in; the struggles and deceits of activities that have not yet reached maturity; the glorious light and happy air with which the new epoch prepares its appearance with flanks open and fiery, with pagan, sweet religion.

(Quien que padezca de lo agrio de la vida en esta comunidad sórdida no ha de comparar a esos deleites el de ver, como hambriento sobre quien cae lluvia de frutas luminosas y aladas, una colección de cuadros sombríos, de esfuerzos del pincel de vistosísimas acumulaciones espirituales, de las batallas a cuyo fragor nació este siglo, de los tanteos y afanes con que engaña su actividad aún no madura, de la gloriosa luz y el aire alegre con que la edad nueva se prepara a animar, con los flancos abiertos y encendidos, la dulce religión pagana.) (1963–1973, 19: 311)

The concepts of combat, the struggle of a dawning new world, an era in which the notions of the past are revived or renewed, are fundamental to Martí's ideology and that of his contemporary modernists. At the same time, these elements establish the bridge between the theoretical formulation of his 1887 essay and the visual symbolism of the poem, all of which is generated in his mind by viewing the Gérome painting. The words of the essay constitute an infrastructure, a verbalization of the norms that the poet will incorporate in his poetry.

In "Pollice verso" the past inserted in the present is evident in the evocation of Martí's period in the penitentiary; "Memory of the Penitentiary" is the subtitle of the poem—a subtitle which leads us to consider one of its principle themes: liberty denied. In this composition, from the very beginning, the poet offers the testimony of a cruel past; and, anticipating combat, he moves us in the direction of denying the spirituality and sensitivity symbolized in the image of "the head bared / of hat and hair" (desnuda la cabeza / De tocado y cabellos; ll. 1–2). He paints for us a vision of personal reality: "And I walked, serenely among vile individuals" (Y yo pasé, sereno entre los viles; l. 9). The memory of past horrors does not deter him. On the contrary, it inspires him to think of the coming battle and the dawning of the "new age": "Memory is a bramble patch; but mine / Is a basket of flames" (Zarzal es la memoria; mas la mía / Es un cesto de llamas; ll. 16–17).

Past and future, taken together, are governed by a new temporality, by a desire for Pythagorean harmony, as the past is renewed in forms that are sometimes joyous but sometimes "harsh and fatal":

> . . . There are laws in the mind, laws
> Like those of the river, the sea, the stone, the star
> Harsh and fatal . . .
>
> (. . . Hay leyes en la mente, leyes
> Cual las del río, el mar, la piedra, el astro
> Asperas y fatales . . .) (ll. 19–20)

Life portrayed in systemized terms is transformed into opposing forces—"bile for the suffering"; "Tokay for the happy." But destiny's face is usually somber:

> . . . Life is somber,—
> A portion of the Universe, a phrase
> Joined to a colossal phrase, . . .
>
> (. . . La vida es grave,—
> Porción del Universo, frase unida
> A frase colossal, . . .) (ll. 36–38)

For those who are frightened or who would like to flee in the face of besieging nightmarish visions, life is:

> A slave tied
> To a golden chariot, which to the very eyes
> Of those it pulls in rapid pace
> Is hidden in the golden dust,—a slave
> With ponderous reins
> Tied to a tireless Eternity!
>
> (. . . sierva ligada
> A un carro de oro, que a los ojos mismos
> De los que arrastra en rápida carrera
> Ocúltese en el áureo polvo,—sierva
> Con escondidas riendas ponderosas
> A la incansable Eternidad atada!) (ll. 40–43)

The vocabulary of suffering of the first section of the poem (verses 1 to 41) prepares the way for the second section in which Martí breathes life into a theme of antiquity with special emphasis upon the battles of this century, as he puts it—mirroring in the process the words of his essay on Gérome.

From line 42 forward the Gérome painting orients the poet: "Life on earth is a circus" (Circo la tierra es; l. 44), an allusion to the Roman circus games, words that are a variation, much as in a musical composition, of the previous words in line 37: "Life is harsh" (La vida es grave). These are two complementary sentences that sum up Martí's frequently melancholy vision of life—his notion that human existence is a disappointment. A third variant appears in line 51: "life is a broad arena" (la vida es la ancha arena). With these three definitions of earth and life, step by step the poet brings us closer to the theme and the language expressed by Gérome in his work. Poetry and painting are conjoined; the poet follows closely the statements of the painter from line 50 on. The visual brushstrokes multiply, recalling Martí's notion that he must see before he writes. And in the poem this visionary creative principle is reflected: "But they look" (Pero miran; l. 53), as well as before: "I fear / seeing" (me aterro / De ver; ll. 12–13), and after, "Oh what an extraordinary visión" (¡Oh qué vision tremenda; l. 75); or "Do you see the chariots . . ." (¿Veis las carrozas . . . ; l. 85); and finally, "See how the foreigners scorn you" (¡Pues ved que los extraños os desdeñan; l. 91).

From lines 48 to 58 Martí adheres to a verbal transposition of the painting. We note there is a complete lack of the physical description of the scene with sensual or chromatic features. In fact, were it not for the inclusion of the words "life is a broad arena" (l. 50), we would have no concrete notion of where the action takes place. To explain the strange nature of the scene we need to return to the poet's characterization of Gérome's painting and take into account the fact that the idea of the canvas fascinated Martí more than the execution of it. Or, stated in another way, Gérome's painting of the theme struck the poet as deficient, and consequently, he concentrated almost exclusively on the concepts he saw in the work and less on the execution. Martí's insistence on the concept is evident in his direct but impassioned discourse. The lines that correspond to the description of the painting lack abundant descriptive adjectives; the sparse characterization serves, in the majority of cases, to sustain and underline the moral, ethical note of the poem, especially the disdain Martí holds for those who surrender easily: coward, lax, servile, lazy are some the adjectives he applies to those who would flee from combat. In support of his accusatory stance is the visual element the poet selects from the canvas—that is, the testimonial value of the public's gaze and that of the king who witness the weakness of the gladiators: "they gaze in silence" (callados miran; l. 53) we read. *Gaze* is a visual verb repeated afterward with emphasis: "But they gaze" (¡Pero miran!; l. 54). This is a gaze that augments the shameful weakness of the oppressed victims of the circus.

The direct transfer of painting to poem is of short duration—nine lines, a further confirmation that the poet's interest is closely tied to a focused viewing of the canvas. In his painting Gérome, via a static and prophetic representation, leaves us suspended as he portrays the vestals making the negative and irrevocable decision of "thumbs down." Martí's message is different; the revolutionary poet is incapable of flinching in the face of his mission to uplift the human spirit and dignify humanity. His personal suffering, expressed in his *Versos libres* never weakens his faith in the future of humankind: "Art [he said] has a single element; and willy nilly, it is directed always to this same element. Its source is human; its objective is always to improve the human lot via emotions; but without the awareness of amelioration" (El Arte tiene un mismo elemento; y sin saberlo, va siempre al mismo objeto. Parte siempre de los hombres; va siempre a mejorar a los hombres por la emoción; sin sentir que mejora) (1963–1978, 19: 420). Thus, Martí felt the need to complete the narration of the painting, to retextualize it. Besides, as we have already noted, Martí believed in metaphysical laws that determine human life and the destiny of both the individual and the nation: "And from the sad earth in which tears are sowed / A tree with tears will sprout. Guilt / Is the mother of punishment" (Y el suelo triste en que se siembran lágrimas, / Dará árbol de lágrimas. La culpa / Es madre del castigo; ll. 31–33). In short, he who allows himself to be defeated suffers the consequences of passivity. The verdict of Gérome's vestals is unacceptable to the poet, who inscribes an alternate message. For him it is imperative to reject the verdict, for in so doing a different destiny is gained. Thus we come to the conclusion of the second section and to the collective agony that the poet as martyr and revolutionary assumes.

The third and final section of "Pollice verso" (ll. 85–92) is devoted to the principle of recovering the past, of demonstrating the existence of parallelism and historical cycles. With special attention to patriotic suffering, Gérome's vision in the second section of the poem is transmuted and becomes a severe exhortation:

> . . . every action is a sign of guilt
> That like a servile ring circles
> A neck, or a generous prize that
> Providentially frees from future ill.
>
> (. . . cada acción es culpa
> Que como aro servil se lleva luego
> Cerrado al cuello, o premio generoso
> Que del futuro mal próvido libra!) (ll. 63–66)

Martí, the visionary, the painter in verse, incorporates the techniques of painting and creates for his oppressed nation a picture of the terrible destiny that is visited upon those who refuse to fight for the liberty of their country. They end up like the weaklings of Gérome's canvas whose detailed visualization is blurred in Martí's indeterminate geography:

> And the guilty row in silence, as if
> Afloat on a sea without water, and they bear
> On their head the yoke of an ox
>
> (Y bogan [los culpable] en silencio, como en magno
> Océano sin agua, y a la frente
> LLevan, cual yugo el buey, la cuerda uncida) (ll. 80–83)

The sensual details abound in this as in the previous section. Luxury is contrasted with the sad destiny of the guilty, the silent, the docile. This contrast of values underlines Martí's painting in verse and, at the same time, it constitutes a commentary on the concept and function of art:

> And the shield of luxurious silver
> And the tiny shoe
> Are at the same time the prison of feet and soul.
> See how the foreigners despise you
> As a despicable race, wretched and lazy!
>
> (Y la albarda de plata suntuosa
> Prendida, y el menudo zapatillo
> Cárcel a un tiempo de los pies y el alma?
> ¡Pues ved que los extraños os desdeñan
> Como raza ruin, menguada y floja) (ll. 88–92)

In the linking of the sections of "Pollice verso" Martí not only combined plastic and literary values but also succeeded in combining them with a harmonious musical sensitivity evident in the tripartite structure of the poem. The three sections suggest the three movements of the sonata form and bring together an organic totality of themes, subthemes, and recapitulations. The themes of suffering, combat and guilt, battle, shame are the motifs of a musical composition. Gérome's canvas suggested the title, but also, in the second section, offers a moment of quiet or peace—much like the second movement of the sonata—and in it Martí joins the past to the present. The first movement and the third are similar in mood:

the third takes up the theme of the first—that is, the suffering and the oppression recounted first from personal experience (ll. 1–17) and then in abstract form (ll. 17–44). The second movement begins with a general note previously announced at the end of the first movement. Upon taking up the thread of the composition in line **X**, third part, the vital note, heralding the dynamism and the exhortative force of the end, acquires an almost strident quality: "Nation, oh, raise your shield . . ." (Alza, oh pueblo el escudo). Then there is a visionary transition (ll. 72–84) and finally the sharp conclusion that restates the theme of guilt of those who choose not to fight for emancipation.

Seen in its totality "Pollice verso" is a representation of the *via crucis* of a creator faced with his destiny and convinced of the power of conquering for Latin America, for Cuba, and for humanity, a new world, an alternative world, distinct from the modernizing bourgeois world around him. To triumph, it was imperative to awaken human consciousness. Hence the importance of this poem in Martí's life and works. It is a call to arms. It is a poem about the future that reads contemporary events. In these visionary lines the anguished modernist poet "painted" a fundamental idea with respect to his own life and that of his nation.

"YESTERDAY I SAW HER . . ."

Martí, the ardent admirer and critic of nineteenth-century painting, was constantly recasting in words the canvases he viewed in New York or Paris art galleries. In Poem XXI of his *Versos sencillos* there is another, but different, example of his transpositional process. It is briefer than that of "Pollice verso," less meditative but more emotional. In the first line of the poem the poet tells us that he is (re)visualizing a canvas recently seen: "Yesterday I saw her in the exhibition" (Ayer la vi en el salon; l. 1). The gallery in question was where, in 1891, an auction of Seney's art collection took place. He tells us in his essay, dated September 2 but published in February of 1891, that among the paintings there was a Jean-Charles Cazin that brings tears to one's eyes (que hace llorar; 164).[7] He does not give us the title of the canvas but does briefly describes it with staccato verbal brushstrokes:

> a peasant family, the mother seated on the grass, with her shawl
> on her shoulders; a child in her arms; the male figure at her
> feet, sleeping, exhausted: his staff nearby; the sky overcast; in
> the distance a house.

> (una familia campesina, la madre sobre la yerba, con el manto
> por los hombros; el niño en sus brazos; el hombre a sus pies,
> dormido, rendido: cerca el bordón; cerrado el cielo; lejos la
> casa.) (164)

Although Martí did not specify the title of the canvas, we now know its title—*Weary Wayfarers*—thanks to Professor Fernández Núñez's research.[8]

The poem is brief—five stanzas with a total of twenty lines. Its emotional impact, however, is intense, and the connection of the poet with the figure of the woman is particularly intimate. In fact, if one were to make a judgment with regard to the nexus between the narrator and his gaze on the basis of the first line—"I saw her yesterday in the exhibition"—one would suspect a sensuous or even an erotic narration in the lines that follow because the stanza ends with the words "My heart skipped a beat" (Se me saltó el corazón; l. 4). But in the following two stanzas the Cuban poet provides a dispassionate description of the scene, which when compared with the canvas is an accurate rendering. But in the stanza that follows, though the transtext continues to display accurate perception, it is obvious that the emotional tone is elevated by dint of negative repetition and the underscoring of elements of *absence* and *anguish*. Nothing described is at variance with the canvas. However, the focus of the transpositional gaze has turned from positive enunciation to selective negation:

> From the barren soil
> Not even a viola or spike is sprouting:
>
> (No nace en el torvo suelo
> Ni una viola, ni una espiga:) (ll. 13, 14)

Followed by two lines contained between exclamation points:

> In the distance, the welcoming cottage,
> The sky very sad and dark! . . .
>
> (¡Muy lejos, la casa amiga,
> Muy triste y oscuro el cielo! . . .) (ll. 15, 16)

The poet's gaze, while not inaccurate in terms of the ekphrastically translated scene, has acquired a symbolic significance—one that dwells upon the dark, anguished side of human experience, a tone that characterizes much of Martí's poetry, especially his *Versos libres*. As in the case of "Pollice verso" there exists a link between art, society, and Martí's reading of modernist institutions and culture. In Poem XXII his heart is touched by the barren existence of these peasants, and he is therefore drawn to the companion of the male peasant in the canvas who labors under adverse conditions. The poet sympathizes with the poor and disadvantaged. His reading of Cazin's canvas echoes other verses of *Versos sencillos*, particularly: "With the wretched of the earth / I want to cast my lot" (Con los pobres de la tierra / Quiero yo mi suerte echar) (16 67). The barren landscape of *Weary Wayfarers* becomes a metaphor for the suffering of the poor and consequently, unlike the case of Gérome's work, the Cuban does not alter the message of the painting. But he is first and foremost attracted to the female figure; her suffering and abnegation touch him so that his poem ends with a repetition of elements of the first stanza:

> That's the beautiful woman
> Who stole my heart yesterday
> In the splendid exhibition
> Of the painters!
>
> (¡Esa es la hermosa mujer
> Que me robó el corazón
> En el soberbio salón
> De los pintores ayer!) (ll. 17–20)

In this brief poem we detect a musical structure not unlike that of "Pollice verso." In sonata form, the first stanza states the theme, the next three contain variations and subthemes, and the final stanza constitutes a recapitulation with thematic variants of the first. Martí, in his experimentation with visual techniques, largely those of the plastic arts, also, consciously or unconsciously, introduced musical structures in his works as we have previously noted in chapter 2 with regard to the impressionistic/expressionistic description of the Hungarian pianist Keleffy's performance in *Lucía Jerez*.[9]

SHADES OF MOREAU

The French writer Joris-Karl Huysmans and his novel *A Rebours* (Against the grain, 1884), the French painter Gustave Moreau, and Julián del Casal

(Cuba, 1863–1893) are linked in the production of the Cuban poet's series of sonnets, *Mi museo ideal* (My ideal museum). Huysmans sent Casal copies of Moreau's expressionist paintings.[10] But Casal's ekphrastic transtexts of Moreau's canvases, insufficiently studied, go beyond literal translation.[11] To illustrate the transformation from canvas to poetry we have chosen Casal's sonnet "Salomé," published in 1890 and based upon a reproduction of the original Moreau painting in Huysmans's *A Rebours*. It was only subsequent to the publication of the sonnet that Casal received copies of Moreau's paintings, sent by Huysmans, and was then able to view for himself the lines and spatial composition of Moreau's *Salomé*.

Oscar Montero in his discussion of *Mi museo ideal* notes that since Casal was not familiar with the original until after the publication of his poem,[12] his transtext of "Salomé" consisted of copying and translating (124), and he adds that precisely for that reason it is attractive "because in the process of reduction, the original is effaced and the subject defines himself *in his own right* . . ." He also considers "Salomé" to be an "*almost* Parnassian" poem, but one in which there is an interplay between the corporal image and its literary representation and between the eroticism of the body and its verbal representation (121). In the genesis of the Moreau representations there is a double ekphrasis of an absent primary canvas: we have Casal's transpositions in his "Museo ideal" and those attempted by Jean Des Esseintes, the protagonist of Huysmans's novel who created his from two Moreau canvases hanging on the walls of his home.

"Salomé" as well as the other sonnets of the "Museo ideal" reflect the Latin American modernist's interest in the descriptive, painterly, sensuous techniques used by the French Parnassians: color, line, contrasts of light and dark, objects of luxury such as precious stones and metals, and the psychological distancing in the literary text between the narrator and the object represented. In Casal's sonnet all of these elements are exemplified, but as Montero has rightly noted, the poem is only "almost" Parnassian. The same can be said of most of the other Latin American modernist poems that were inspired by the theoretical ideas of the French Parnassians and their prose and poetry texts.[13] Casal's sonnet reads as follows:

> In the Hebrew palace, where the soft
> Fragrant smoke dissolved by the sun
> Rises and disappears into the limestone ceiling
> Or is dispersed in the broad nave;

> The Tetrarch sits with solemn gaze
> With gray beard and emaciated chest,
> He sits on his throne, impassive and erect,
> As if lulled by the songs of birds.
>
> Before him, with a brocaded vestment
> Studded with sparkling jewels
> To the sweet sound of a sonorous mandolin
>
> Salomé dances, and raised in her right hand
> She continues to display, radiant with joy,
> A white lotus with golden pistils.
>
> (En el palacio hebreo, donde el suave
> humo fragante, por el sol deshecho,
> sube a perderse en el calado techo
> o se dilata en la anchurosa nave;
>
> está el Tetrarca de mirada grave
> barba canosa y extenuado pecho,
> sobre el trono, hierático y derecho,
> como adormido por canciones de ave.
>
> Delante de él, con veste de brocado
> estrellada de ardiente pedrería,
> al dulce son del bandolín sonoro,
>
> Salomé baila y en la diestra alzado,
> muestra siempre, radiante de alegría,
> un loto blanco de pistilos de oro.) (173–174)

These sonnets as well as the larger corpus of Casal's poems and his recently collected prose pieces over the years have had an unfortunately traditional reading that more often than not has defined his art as escapist, sensuous, Parnassian, or romantic.[14] But with the work of critics such as Montero it is clear we need to reread Casal's poetry and prose, revise our critical evaluations of his work, and, specifically, examine the links of his often ambiguous discourse, which contains embedded modernist enunciations, both erotic and sociopolitical elements. Our arguments are double-pronged: 1) If we reread Casal's *crónicas*[15] dealing with the society of Havana in which he describes the corrupt, fetid, decadent state of colonial Cuba we can no longer consider the Cuban to be an escapist who creates his art enclosed in an ivory tower. And, 2), in light of the social and political commentaries of his essays, the so-called escapist analyses of his poems, especially the sonnets of his "Museo ideal," call for a revisionist interpretation. Not only are they painterly in execution, but the constant luxurious "covering" of the figures and their searching of spatial horizons more than a French Parnassian influence suggest the presence of both an erotic and political subtext.

In the ekphrastic rendering of the Moreau painting, Casal presents us from the first line with a distancing two historical figures—Salomé and Herod—whose presence embodies a symbolic statement, both in the original and in the Cuban version: the imperative of creating an alternate reality, which in Casal's case, constitutes a replacement, a varnishing intended to conceal the island's decadent colonial reality. It is a spatial transfer common to other modernists' texts that Cintio Vitier has rejected as an evasion[16] and described as the need to create an alternative universe among the modernists, who sought to redefine their reality and their role within it. In Casal's sonnet the narration has a note of distance from the first line forward. It also suggests a move toward dispersal (a symbolic suggestion of resituation?) in the image of the smoke that is scattered by the rays of the sun. The dynamics of the first quatrain is replaced by immobility in the second: Herod sits immobile, pensive, half-asleep, lulled by the music of the birds. The final tercets echo and embellish the dynamic gaze of the opening lines. The glitter of Parnassian luxury is described before we know it belongs to the figure of Salomé, who appears dancing at the very end of the poem. Moreau's gaze is transferred by Casal as does the reader, "invited" into the "ideal museum." Both view the scene from the sidelines, suggesting their role as voyeurs of an ambiguous reality that overlays the crass and vulgar reality of nineteenth-century societal transitions. In Casal's case the depiction of the lotus, a phallic totem, constitutes a symbolic veil, much like Salomé's. In other Moreau and Casal texts, it is a veil that goes beyond sensuality and suggests the erotic/gay subtext of Casal's works, which Montero has skillfully uncovered for today's readers of Casal's art.

ADDENDUM

Pollice verso
(Memoria de presidio)

Sí! Yo también, desnuda la cabeza
De tocado y cabellos, y al tobillo
Una cadena lurda, heme arastrado
Entre un montón de sierpes, que revueltas
Sobre sus vicios negros, parecían   5
Esos gusanos de pesado vientre
Y ojos viscosos que en hedionda cuba
De pardo lodo lentos se revuelcan!
Y yo pasé, sereno entre los viles.
Cual si en mis manos, como en ruego juntas,   10
Las anchas alas púdicas, se abriese
Una paloma blanca. Y aun me aterro
De ver con el recuerdo lo que he visto
Una vez con mis ojos. Y espantado,
Póngome en pie, cual a emprender la fuga!—¡Recuerdos hay
    que queman la memoria!   15
¡Zarzal es la memoria; mas la mía
Es un cesto de llamas! A su lumbre
El porvenir de mi nación preveo.
Y lloro. Hay leyes en la mente, leyes
Cual las del río, el mar, la piedra, el astro.   20
Asperas y fatales: ese almendro
Que con su rama oscura en flor sombrea
Mi alta ventana, viene de semilla
De almendro; y ese rico globo de oro
De dulce y perfumoso jugo lleno   25
Que en blanca fuente una niñuela cara,
Flora del destierro, cándida me brinda,
Flor del destierro, cándida me brinda,
Naranja es, y vino de naranjo:—
Y el suelo triste en que se siembran lágrimas,   30
Dará árbol de lágrimas. La culpa
Es madre del castigo.
No es la vida
Copa de mago que el capricho torna

En hiel para los míseros, y en férvido   35
Tokay para el feliz: La vida es grave,—
Porción del Universo, frase unida
A frase colosal, sierva ligada
A un carro de oro, que a los ojos mismos
De los que arrastra en rápida Carrera   40
Ocúltase en el áureo polvo,—sierva
Con escondidas riendas ponderosas
A la incansable Eternidad atada!

Circo la tierra es, como el Romano,
Y junto a cada cuna una invisible   45
Panoplia al hombre aguarda, donde lucen,
Cual daga cruel que hiere al que la blande,
Los vicios, y cual límpidos escudos
Las virtudes: la vida es la ancha arena,
Y los hombres esclavos gladiadores,—   50
Mas el pueblo y el rey, callados miran
De grada excelsa, en la desierta sombra.
¡Pero miran! Y a aquel que en la contienda
Bajó el escudo, o lo dejó de lado,
O suplicó cobarde, o abrió el pecho   55
Laxo y servil a la enconosa daga
Del enemigo, las vestales rudas
Desde el sitial de la implacable piedra,
Condenan a morir, *pollice verso,*
Y hasta el pomo ruin la daga hundida,   60
Al flojo gladiador clava en la arena.

¡Alza, oh pueblo, el escudo, porque es grave
Cosa esta vida, y cada acción es la culpa
Que como aro servil se lleva luego
Cerrado al cuello, o premio gneroso   65
Que del futuro mal próvido libra.

¿Veis los esclavos? Como cuerpos muertos
Atados en racimo, a vuestra espalda
Irán vida tras vida, y con las frentes
Pálidas y angustiosas, la sombría   70
Carga en vano halaréis, hasta que el viento

De vuestra pena bárbara apiadado,
¡Oh, qué vision tremenda! ¡Oh qué terrible
Los átomos postreros evapore!
Procesión de culpables! Como en llano   75
Negro los miro, torvos, anhelosos,
Sin fruta el arbolar, secos los píos
Bejucos, por comara fueraria
Donde ni el sol da luz, ni el árbol sombra!
Y bogan en silencio, como en magno   80
Océano sin agua, y a la frente
LLevan, cual yugo el buey, la cuerda uncida,
Y a la zaga, listado el cuerpo flaco
De hondos azotes, el montón de siervos!

¿Véis las carrozas, las ropillas blancas   85
Risueñas y ligeras, el luciente
Corcel de crin trenzada y riendas ricas,
Y la albarda de plata suntuosa
Prendida, y el menudo zapatillo
Cárcel a un tiempo de los pies y el alma?   90
¡Pues ved que los extraños os desdeñan
Como a raza ruin, menguada y floja!

Pollice verso (Thumbs Down)
(Prison Memoir)

Yes!
I, too, with shaven head, my ankles chained,
Have dragged myself through knots of snakes
Writhing in their filth like bloated worms
Squirming in a bed of foul, brown mud.
I calmly made my way among the base
As if between my hands, clasped as in prayer,
A snow-white dove were opening her wings.
I shudder yet to see in reverie
Scenes I have witnessed with my very eyes—
I leap in fear as if to run away!
Images that sear the memory!
Memory's a burning bush, but mine's a flame

By whose gleaming light I can foresee
The future of my nation. And I weep.
Because the mind has laws, just like the stone,
The river, and the star. Harsh laws, and firm:
The almond tree, whose flowering boughs now shade
My lofty window, sprang from an almond seed.
And this rich globe of gold (so full of sweet
And fragrant juice), now kindly served to me
By a child, dear daughter of exile,
Upon a gleaming platter, is an orange,
Fruit of the orange tree. The mournful groan
Where human tears are sown can nothing bear
Except a tree of tears. Guilt, likewise,
Engenders punishment. This life is not
A wizard's brew, becoming at a whim
Gall for the damned, but for the fortunate few
A sparkling Tokay. No, life is grave:
Part of the universe—one phrase
Of a colossal whole; a slave hitched
To a golden chariot that clouds the eyes
Of those who ride in it with golden dust—
A slave whose hidden reins are linked
To all eternity.
          Life is a circus
Like the Roman one. By every newborn's crib
There is a panoply—invisible—
Whose shadowy gleams illumine and foretell,
Like a shining sword that cruelly wounds
The one who wields it, all the future
Failings of the man. But, like bright shields,
All his future virtues gleam there too.
Life's the great arena; men are but
The gladiator slaves. And from the stands
The king and people watch—in silence—
But they watch! The fighter in the fray
Who lowers a shield or tosses it aside,
Who makes a coward's plea, or cringing low,
Bares his breast to receive the enemy sword
Is surely doomed. The vestal virgins
Seated in honor on implacable rock

Harshly condemn the cowardly to die.
They sentence death, *pollice verso*;
The sword then plunges to its sorry hilt
And pins the gladiator to the sand.

Oh people, raise your shields, for life is real!
And each act an offense, which like a ring
Soon hangs about our necks, or else a generous deed
That has the power to ward off future ills.
Do you see the slaves? Like bodies of the dead
Tied one to one, they march behind our backs
Life after life, their foreheads pale with grief,
The dark and dreadful burden we must drag
Until the wind, compassionate, dries up
The final atoms of our barbarous crime.
Oh, vision of despair! How terrible to see
The long procession of the damned. Behold
Them, grim, upon a dismal plain,
A fruitless orchard or withered stand of reeds—
Funereal land where trees withhold their shade,
And the sun, her blessed light. In silence now
They trudge as if across an endless,
Waterless sea. In front of them they bear
As oxen bear their yoke, the dreaded chain.
Behind, their wretched backs are striped
From lashes that have cut into the flesh—
The mass of slaves!
See the carriages?
White raiment, soft and light, the gleaming
Stallion's braided mane and splendid reins?
The saddle of sumptuous silver, that tiny shoe
Confining foot and soul? Well, behold!
Strangers scorn you as a cowardly race!

—Translated by Jo Anne Engelbert

4

FACING THE ORIENT

In desultory notes, paralleling Jules Michelet's statement that "the Orient advances, invincible, fatal to the gods of light by the charm of its dreams, by the magic of its *chiaroscuro*" (quoted by Said, 73), José Martí, declared that "the Orient invades the West" (El Oriente invade el Occidente) (1963–1973, 19: 359) not merely in the context of nineteenth-century discursive practice, including ekphrastic textualizations, but as a sign of hybridity in the evolution of the interplay of East-West culture.

In reexamining Spanish American modernist texts that span the years 1880 to 1930 and in which the Orient is inscribed, in this chapter we will argue that 1) there is a need to question the perpetuation of previous critical positions with regard to the meaning of Orientalism in modernist literature; and 2) that the revisioning of modernism's Orientalisms implies a fundamentally dynamic project in which the nineteenth-century's desire for the Orient should be viewed not simply "as an *intertextual* phenomenon but . . . as a social phenomenon" (Behdad, 136), a visualization process that is scripted into a network of heterogeneous cultural representations generated by the forces of both authority and aesthetics. Furthermore, if we prefer to speak of *Orientalisms* rather than Orientalism it is because of the heterogeneous, polyphonic nature of a discourse referring to both Near and Far East whose basic operational meaning we appropriate from Edward Said: "Orientalism [he insists] is the discipline by which the Orient was (and is) approached systematically, as a topic of learning, discovery, and practice" (73).

In the course of this process of learning, discovery, and practice the Spanish American modernists were drawn to the representations of the

53

Orient they encountered in their readings of classical and nineteenth-century texts (principally French) and reproductions of Oriental art. With respect to readings, an insight into their contemporary archive can be gleaned from a narration by Abel Morán, the protagonist of Efrén Rebolledo's short novel *Hojas de bambú* (Bamboo leaves). Morán had read

> the *Book of Wonders* in which the master Marco Polo spoke for the first time of distant Cipango [China], goading, with his vivid descriptions the studies of wise men and at the same time feeding the greed of the conquerors . . . ; the studies on *Japanese Art* of Edmund de Goncourt and Gonse . . . ; the novels of Loti . . . ; the *Japanese Histories*, by the magnificent Lafcadio Hearns, each one of whose lines is a gem of literature.[1]

> (el *Libro de las maravillas*, en que Maese Marco Polo habló por primera vez del distante Cipango, aguijoneando, con sus vívidas descripciones, la aplicación de los sabios a la par que la codicia de los conquistadores. . . . los estudios sobre el *Arte Japonés* de Edmundo de Goncourt y de Gonse . . . ; las novelas de Loti . . . ; las *Historias japonesas*, cada una de cuyas líneas es una joya de literatura.) (178)

Inspired by these and other cultural readings, instead of directing his steps toward the more traditional choice of exploring Europe, Morán preferred to feast his eyes, firsthand, on prototypical Oriental visions: "cricket cages and dwarf pines, houses made of paper and geishas with colorful kimonos and dark hair buns, temples of red lacquer, the graceful Fujiyama and Japanese natural settings of blue skies and twisted trees" (178). It was the lure of exotic scenery, fueled by the sense of an ending that moved him and other protagonists to examine the Orient: that is, an awareness that tourism and European colonialism had already turned what was exotic into the familiar. Thus, as Behdad notes, the belated travel writers and literary artists of the nineteenth century, filled with the desire to explore alternative horizons, other cultures, and cognitive systems, frustrated in their desire to capture an authentic Other, produced melancholy discourses, texts signifying an absence, frequently taking as present what in fact had already vanished (92).

This loss of the past is inserted in many forms in modernist texts; we find it, for example, in Martí's *Versos sencillos* (1963–1973, 16: 120), framed in the symbolic statement of Agar's frustrated search for her lost pearl. Or in Gómez Carrillo's polarized vision of Damascus, which, much to his chagrin, he discovers is a modern city. However, a visit to the old part of the city where he finds houses are hermetic, hostile, and mysterious intrigues him in his search for the traditional, paradigmatic Orient (Gómez Carrillo 152–153). There is in his writing a splitting or refraction of Orientalist discursive authority, that is, an ambivalence and uncertainty evident in his search for the *true* Orient, on the one hand, and the discovery of its absence, on the other, as he slowly realizes the past is irretrievable. In spite of these contradictions, characteristic of the hegemonic Orientalist discourse, or perhaps because of them, his Orientalism is frequently lacking in cultural distortion or fanciful idealizations. It contains what Said would term an unrepresentative "natural" depiction (21) evidenced, for example, when Gómez Carrillo writes that the Orient is on the cusp of modernization or that China is a working industrial country. And as he travels from Near East to Far East, his gaze is not that of the colonizer but of a Westerner who chronicles the steps taken by the Orient in its process of industrialization. Thus, he notes that Shanghai is the most Western of the Chinese ports (178) in a country that only a few years before was a place where the production of anything other than products of ivory, lacquer, silk, or porcelain, seemed impossible (176–177). In the face of modernity's displacement of tradition, his, like that of other modernists, is a search for value in the face of the rationalization and secularization of society from the time of the French Revolution and the spread of the market system in nineteenth-century capitalist societies. Traditional societies with fixed, frequently hierarchical social constructions had no need to search for value; value became visible and significant only at the point at which it ceased to exist, that is, with the advent of modernity. "In the passage from the traditional to the rationalized, value is at once lost (as reality) and gained (as abstraction)" (Bongie, 8). And so he, together with other modernists, cultivates an exoticizing strategy by selecting and focusing upon Oriental visions such as the mysterious *musmé* he glimpses as he leaves the train station in Tokyo, an embodiment of the Orientalized Orient, the stereotypical sensual, seductive, eccentric, impenetrable, and fatalistic reconstruction of the voids of the present.[2] The *musmé* is presented as a painted portrait, colored with pale yellow and white as if she were a deity of one of Botticelli's paintings. Her eyes, painted for readers are

> not big but long, very narrow and very long, [and] have a volup
> tuous sweetness that explains the enthusiasm of those ancient

Japanese poets who composed *tankas* in which women's pupils are compared to filters of enchantment. . . . And this spirit does not wear the gray unadorned dress of my female traveling companions, but a pale yellow kimono covered with white lilies that makes her appear to be a deity of spring of this nation, smaller and more splendid than that of Botticelli, but no less seductive. I contemplate her entranced.

(no grandes [sino] largos, muy estrechos y muy largos, tienen una dulzura voluptuosa que explica el entusiasmo de aquellos antiguos poetas nipones que compusieron las tankas en que las pupilas femeninas son comparadas con filtros de encantamiento. . . . Y esta aparición no lleva el traje gris sin adornos de mis compañeros de viaje, sino un kimono amarillo pálido, cubierto de lirios blancos que la hacen parecer como una Primavera de esta tierra, más menuda y menos espléndida que la de Botticelli, pero no menos seductora. Yo la contemplo absorto.) (Gómez Carrillo 185)

Darío alluded to this fascination in his prologue to Gómez Carrillo's *De Marsella a Tokio* (From Marseilles to Tokyo): "This poet, I say, comes from the country of dragons, of rare things, of awesome landscapes and of people who seem to have fallen from the moon" (Este poeta, me digo, viene del país de los dragones, de las cosas raras, de los paisajes milagrosos y de las gentes que parecen caídas de la luna) (Tanabe, 27n37). "He was attracted by all things strange or unknown, and demonstrated a violent seduction for a young girl who knew nothing of Western nations or other ways of thinking" (Tanabe, 27).

Why, we may well ask, this transfixion with Orientalized Orients in modernist discourse? What lies beneath the more obvious textual surfaces of these "exotic" appropriated gazes? What are the modalities of modernism's Oriental discourse? Is it, as Abdeslam Azougarth has suggested, a counterdiscursive mechanism for dealing with a developing mercantilist society whose newly instituted norms and values nineteenth-century Latin American writers found to be at odds with their cultural, social, and aesthetic ideals? Or is it a case of the writers' protesting against the values of an economic modernity that denied art its previously accepted role as a determination of truth and spirituality (Azougarth 13–14)? In response, did the modernists, in their conflictive relationship with modernity, choose the path of evasion and geographical displacement that the Orient, among other imagined spaces and communities, provided with its voluptuous plastic visions of sultans, peris, Scheherazades, Aladdins, pagodas, temples, kimonos, and cherry blossoms? In engaging these issues, Zavala posits the notion that among the modernists the utilitarianism and disintegration of established social paradigms encouraged the creation of supernaturalisms, the experience of the occult and the esoteric. It also heightened subjectivities beyond the boundaries of reason and "acted as a mechanism for dealing with or mediating social contradictions . . ." (Zavala 127). However, the question of hegemonic authority so uppermost in Said's perception of Orientalism "as a sign of European-Atlantic power over the Orient [rather] than . . . a 'true' discourse about the Orient" (6) is called into question by Kushigian, for example, whose view is that Hispanic Orientalism, unlike its French or British models, is not repressive or manipulative but an open and welcoming means of exploring the self through a gaze upon the Other (12). If, in the face of these multiple and conflicting concepts we proceed from theory to praxis by analyzing the alternative spaces of modernism's Orientalism in Julio Herrera y Reissig's exemplary poem "Odalisca" (Odalisque) (*Las clepsidras*, 1910), we may succeed in clarifying the function and meaning of *exoticism*, so essential to the concept of a painted Orientalism and the nature of its discursive operation:

Odalisque

To bewitch me, houri of marvels,
you startled me with oriental pomp,
with earrings, slippers, veils and corals,
with bangles and astral necklaces.

On regal carpets, on hands and knees,
you smoked the hookah with ritualistic opiums,
while to the sound of gusles and drums
the aromatic incense burned.

Your body, undulating in the Turkish manner,
slipped into a mystical mazurka . . .
Then in a waltz of strange gyrations

you vanished in a miraculous haze,
carried away by chimeras of smoke
above the glory of the censer.

(Odalisca)

> Para hechizarme, hurí de maravillas,
> Me sorprendiste en pompas orientales,
> De aros, pantuflas, velos y corales,
> Con ajorcas y astrales gargantillas . . .
>
> Sobre alcatifas regias, en cuclillas,
> Gustataste el narguilé de opios rituales
> Mientras al son de guzlas y timables
> Ardieron aromáticas pastillas.
>
> Tu cuerpo, ondeando a la manera turca,
> Se insinuó en una mística mazurka . . .
> Luego en un vals de giros extranjeros
>
> Te evaneciste en milagroso esfumo,
> Arrebatada por quimeras de humo,
> Sobre la Gloria de los pebeteros.) (280)

Herrera's exploration of Oriental plastic beauty constitutes a displacement in space in which the narrator is entranced and overpowered by the ravishing houri. In a prototypical representation his gaze is centered upon the female body, which in the final tercet dissolves into the smoke and fumes of the incense pot. In examining Herrera's exoticism Said's two methodological devices seem particularly appropriate: *strategic location*, that is, "the author's position in a text with regard to the Oriental material he writes about," and *strategic formation*, "the relationship between texts and the way in which groups of texts, types of texts, even textual genres, acquire mass, density, and referential power among themselves and thereafter in the culture at large" (20). In "Odalisque" as in other Orientalist poems by Herrera ("Oleo Indostánico," "Unción Islamita") the poet paints the Orient via a reinscription as part of a process of definition of both self and the universe. Emphasis is on the visual, which is conveyed through creative, experimental metaphors. The female body, the center of his focus, rises to the level of a metaphor of the Orient and suggests a strategic formation that is not only self-referential but socially mediated—a reconceptualization dynamically formed and frequently deformed. Herrera's representation of women in enticing idealized poses—a prototype of the stereotyped modernist vision of the Oriental female body—is not "an innocent depiction of the beauty of exotic peoples but an ethnographic alibi arising from the desire to create a sexual text that can be manipulated, interpreted, and exchanged between artist, exotic subjects, and spectators" (Charnon-Deutsch, 252).[3] The poet's exoticism is not merely an aesthetic exercise; it is tied to his role as a *voyeur*; it reflects hierarchical social and culturally generated positions of masculine and feminine values. And in privileging difference it serves to explore what is both threatening and necessary to male subjectivity (Charnon-Deutsch, 254). A progression of generative factors, based on Mario Praz's ideas, would seem to be operational here: curiosity and desire to fathom the unknown leads to exoticism; the desire for distant cultures produces a flight from self and ultimately eroticism (Tanabe, 43), as we have seen in the previous discussion (chapter 3) of Casal's "Salomé." In its broader social connotations, the Orient, metaphorized in the female body, is perceived as a sexually unstable, mysterious, impenetrable space, and as such, its representations are not only cultural or aesthetic but political. Kabbani says the insistence on the portrayal of women is linked to the dominant culture's patriarchal values and its racism. The female other is seen as a member of a subgroup in patriarchal society, and Oriental women were doubly demeaned—as women and as Orientals—while at the same time they were sublimated (67).

Revisionist analyses of so-called modernist escapist discourses, Orientalist or other, have taught us that when examined as a corpus they constitute social texts that through a strategy of geographic or cultural displacement are linked to a social and political agenda in spite of the fact that as individual texts they can be—and frequently are—(mis)read as mere aestheticizing enunciations of idealized visions conjured up by the writer's creative spirit. A binary strategy of reading texts—aesthetic and sociocultural—can be applied in "Odalisque" to the stereotypical artifacts of the focused gaze upon the houri's slippers, earring, or veils. The veil in particular attracts the eye and forces us to speculate about what is behind it. It hides the woman but heightens the voyeur's desire for penetration and knowledge. The inscription of the veil turns the Oriental woman, a synecdoche of Oriental culture, into an enigma. We are reminded of Casal's sensuous ekphrasis of Salomé, dancing, bejeweled to the sound of sweet music with a white lotus in her hand ("Salomé," 173). "In Western eyes, the Orient is always *more and other* than what it appears to be, for it always and everywhere appears in a veiled, disguised, and deceptive manner" (Yegenoglu, 48). The veil, visualized and described graphically, not only hides but reveals—travelers, writers, or poets establish via the veil an imaginary anchor in order to assert individual subjectivity and authority (Yegenoglu, 48). Authority for Latin American writers, notes Zavala, was different from European figurations that sought to construct the Orient as Other while establishing national identities. Rather than a discourse of power to create, incorporate, or control Oriental spaces, Latin American writers sought to affirm their own identities through discourses *against* power (Zavala 85) created through creolized visions, plastic transpositions, and polyphonic hybridized strategies. In Herrera's poem this pluriculturalism is evidenced in the houri's dancing of the mazurka and the waltz, the latter character-ized by the narrator as a waltz of strange—that is, foreign—gyrations. The orchestration and juxtaposition of these non-Oriental objects and artifacts are linked to a strategy of appropriation whose desired end product is the recreation of self and the liberation of the social community from center-imposed cultural and sociopolitical systems during the period of emerging national cultures in nineteenth-century Latin America.

Reinscription need not follow the *self-other modality* as in Herrera's work. It can also be inscribed from within, either through "natural" (Said's term) enunciations such as those in Martí's chronicles or in aesthetic for-mulations such as those of Tablada's appropriated haikus. In the case of Martí's writing, the hand of the revolutionary is evident in his reporting of the upheavals and rebellions in Egypt in the 1880s sparked by the Egyp-tians longing to free themselves of the presence of the English and the threats of the French: "Egypt [he wrote] finds that that it has paid too dearly the civilization and the support which it asked of the Europeans and it wants to throw off the yoke of its civilizers" (Egipto halla que ha pagado demasiado caro la civilización y el apoyo que pidió a los europeos, y quiere lanzar de sí a los civilizadores) (1963–1973, 23: 158). Indochina has similar aspirations, he writes in one of his children's stories published in *La edad de oro* (The golden age):

> We wear pigtails, pointed hats, wide breeches, colored shirts, and we are yellow, short, frail and ugly; but we work with both bronze and silk: and when the French came to take away our Hanoi, our Hue, our cities with wood palaces, our ports with their houses of bamboo and boats made of reeds, our storehous-es of fish and rice, in spite of our almond-shaped eyes, we knew how to die, thousands and thousands of us died in order to close off their approach. Now they are our masters; but tomor-row, who knows!

(Usamos moño, y sombrero de pico, y calzones anchos, y blusón de color, y somos amarillos, chatos, canijos y feos; pero trabajamos a la vez el bronce y la seda: y cuando los franceses nos han venido a quitar nuestro Hanoi, nuestro Hue, nuestras ciudades de palacios de madera, nuestros puertos llenos de casas de bambú y de barcos de junco, nuestros almacenes de pescado y arroz, todavía, con estos ojos de almendra, hemos sabido morir, miles sobre miles, para cerrarles el camino. Ahora son nuestros amos; pero mañana ¡quién sabe!) (1963–1973, 18: 461–462)

Martí's is an internalized Oriental discourse, and though "natural" in Said's schema, it is replete with detailed graphics—bronze, silk, boats, reeds, fish. It is a discourse generated not by hegemonic authority but by the Orient's search for authenticity in a projected, liberated, and reconstructed sociopolitical community. It is, in addition, a discourse that exemplifies the open, welcoming Orientalism described by Kushigian (11–12). It frequently seeks guidance from the East:

From the Arabs we should take two things at least: their daily prayer in which they ask Allah to help them choose an unswerving course,—and their proverb which asserts that he who turns his head when dogs thwart his path will not reach the end of his journey.

(Del árabe se han de tomar dos cosas a lo menos: su oración de todos los días, en que pide a Allah que le haga ir por camino recto,—y el proverbio aquel que dice que no llegará al final de su jornada el que vuelva la cabeza a los perros que le salgan al camino.) (1963–1973, 3: 117).

The appropriation of these Oriental adages is inserted into Martí's political discourse and his revolutionary project for Cuba's liberation from Spanish rule. But his can also be a decorative, aesthetic discourse, as we have noted in our discussion of the decorative art objects in *Lucía Jerez* (18: 205), in his insistent use of the metaphor of Arab steeds (e.g., 1963–1973, 17: 270), in his reference to the "mushma" [*sic*] in *Versos sencillos*, or in lines from an erotic poem that conjure up parallel visions of *ukiyo-e* prints:[4]

> Over her delicate ear
> Her voluptuous hair falls
> Like a curtain
> Which rises near her neck.
> The ear is a heavenly creation
> Of Chinese porcelain.
>
> (Por sobre la oreja fina
> Baja lujoso el cabello,
> Lo mismo que una cortina
> Que se levanta hacia el cuello.
> La oreja es obra divina
> De porcelana de China.) (1963–1973, 16: 121)

But it is José Juan Tablada rather than Martí who among the modernists is most consistently and ardently identified with the Oriental. Tablada was not the first Spanish American modernist to cultivate Oriental themes. That distinction rests with Casal, especially in his celebrated poems "Sourimono" or "Kakemono," whose original title was "Pastel Japonés" (A Japanese pastel), signaling the significant role painting, ceramics, and sculpture played in the creation of an Oriental literary discourse in nineteenth-century Spanish America. It has been said Tablada's Orientalism—gleaned from French readings and the plastic arts as well as, firsthand, from his travels in the East—conceived of the Orient as a literary circumstance, a formalist disfigurement lacking in hybridity, correlation, or affinity vis-à-vis national or regional cultural identities (Schneider in Rebolledo, 9). Those who fault Tablada for his lack of a national sensibility point out the futility of his attempting to use an Oriental form—the *hai-kai*—in a Western idiom (Schneider in Rebolledo, 9). But Tablada was aware of the tensions of his cultural preferences. In the poem "Exégesis" he elucidates the nature of the doubleness of his discourse with the sensuous images associated with an Oriental gaze gleaned in large measure from painterly, plastic sources and populated with Buddhas, lotuses, jades, brocades, and cherry trees:

> My soul, a hieroglyphic, is both Mexican and Asian.
> . . . . . .
>
> Perhaps my mother when she bore me in her womb
> Looked at many Buddhas, lotuses, the magnificent

Nippon art and everything those strange boats
Off-loaded on the native shores of the Pacific!

That's why I love jades, smaragdine stones,
The light green *chalchihuitl*, with its double mystery,
For it decorated monarchs of Anahuac and China
And it germinates only in Mexico and the Celestial Empire.

Wrapped in the sumptuous brocades of the Seres
And adorned with jades, my poetic inspiration is American,
And in the onyx vessel that is my heart,
Endowing my blood with its esoteric vigor,
Flowers a miraculous
Japanese cherry tree!

(Es de México y de Asia mi alma un jeroglífico
. . . . . .

¡Quizá mi madre cuando me llevó en sus entrañas
Miró mucho los budas, los lotos, el magnífico
Arte nipón y todo cuanto las naos extrañas
Volcaron en las playas natales del Pacífico.

Por eso amo los jades, la piedra esmaragdiña,
El verdegay chalchíhuitl, por su doble misterio,
Pues ornó a los monarcas de Anáhuac y de China
Y solo nace en México y en el Celeste Imperio.

Envuelto en los suntuosos brocados de Sérica
Y exornado de jades, mi numen es de América,
Y en el vaso de ónix que es mi corazón,
Infundiendo a mi sangre su virtud esotérica,
Florece un milagroso
Cerezo de Japón) (1953, 69)

The Mexican poet, who described himself as a "servant of the Mikado"
and a bonze of the Orient's pagodas ("Japón," in Tablada 1904, 121), was a
lifelong devotee of Japanese culture, which he wove into his texts from his
first volume of poetry, *El florilegio*, and especially in the second, 1904, edition with its section of "Poemas exóticos" (Exotic poems) and his "Musa

japónica" (Japanese muse). The 1904 edition also includes translations of *utas* and a section of "Cantos de amor y de otoño" (Songs of love and fall), which paraphrase short texts of the *Kokinshifu*, a collection of ancient and modern Japanese odes. In prose he is known for his journalistic pieces, written while in Japan, that were later collected under the title of *El país del sol* (The land of the sun). If in the first period of his work (1890–1900) there is an attraction to exotic themes, French learned and inspired, in the second (1900–1902) there is a movement toward authenticity in place of exoticism. The third period (1911–1920), the period when he travels to France to expand his knowledge of the Orient, also includes the period of his stay in New York where he internationalizes his creative and cultural insights, befriends the Japanese scholar Frederick Starr, and publishes his essay on the Japanese painter Hiroshige, whose art had an overwhelming significance on Tablada's most significant, original Japanesque poetry— including his experiments in melding rhythm and spatial dimension with poetic discourse. First came the *hai-kais* in a steady stream:

> Bits of mud
> On the darkened path
> Frogs jump . . .
>
> (Trozos de barro,
> Por la senda en penumbra
> Saltan los sapos . . .) (1953, 82)

and then, more daring innovations, inspired by Japanese calligraphy, by the transfer of techniques from the print media, especially those of Hiroshige. Through his experiments Tablada succeeded in creating visual rhythm—before its use by either Vicente Huidobro or Octavio Paz. In Japanese calligraphy and art he discovered transferable techniques to produce poetry that would simplify, symbolize, and synthesize impressions and voices. In his book on Hiroshige, Tablada indicated he used "japanism as a springboard to awaken among Mexican artists an interest in popular national art. He was not an exoticist, clear and simple, as other Modernists" (138). This emphasis upon the plastic arts—calligraphy or Hiroshige's prints—suggests, as we noted at the start of this chapter, the need to reconsider previous critical positions that have identified the genesis of Hispanic Orientalism with literary texts, especially at the start, with those of the Goncourts or Loti. But the plastic arts were equally significant in creating a Latin American Oriental discourse. Tablada, for example, explained that before his trip to Japan he collected Japanese paintings in reproductions, including *Fugaku Hiakei* by Hokusai. His interest in erotic poetry was stimulated by viewing *ukiyo-e* prints, representations of sexual union in which the male organ was drawn in an incredibly exaggerated size and female faces expressed complete ecstasy.

Tablada's ties to art were both visual and literary: he read Goncourt's works on the Japanese artists Utamaro (1891) and Hokusai (1896) (Tanabe 37) and admired their works. Utamaro's influence was especially notable, not only on Tablada, but on other modernists whose texts evidence a transference of pictorial elements to literary imagistic systems. In general, the modernists were captivated by an art form that in the Orient was considered unorthodox and decadent, that is, the art of painters who represented Oriental women as we find them in so many modernist texts: white faces, eyes narrow as threads, small mouths like a cherry tree leaf, inexpressive and indolent but with the suggestion that behind their mysterious impassivity was an insatiable passion.[5] And while it is true that most modernists were not as well acquainted with Oriental art as Tablada, we know, for example, that Casal, in the case of the sonnets of *Mi museo ideal* (My ideal museum), appropriated biblical themes he found in reproductions of Gustave Moreau's canvases and that he was moved in "Japonerías" (Japanese bibelots) by the sight, one morning, of the splendor of a Japanese ceramic.[6] We also know that Martí was fascinated by Oriental art to the point of translating an essay by Em. Bergerat on Japanese painting, which reviews the different forms of art cultivated by the Japanese and their historical development (1963–1973, 19: 321–326). In short, in can be said that the engendering sources of modernist Orientalisms were the written word of literary texts and art criticism (principally French), paintings, and the decorative arts. And while exoticism stands out as the sharper of their discursive modalities, it should not be taken at face value. The examination of modernism's Oriental *strategic formations* confirms ever-present emancipatory projections and epistemological concerns linked to the reconstruction of self, the nation, and the universe.

5

WRITERS AS ART CRITICS

The modernization of Latin American literary texts that began in the 1870s was, as we have already noted, a socioeconomic and aesthetic process that resulted in the transference of techniques observed in the visual arts and their application to discursive practices in both prose and poetry. A synaesthetic relationship between literature and painting permeated theoretical statements, stray notebook entries, poetry and prose texts and led to the creation of a chromatic literary palette as well as to the incorporation of the impressionistic and expressionistic experiments cultivated by European artists in the late nineteenth century. Writers in a sense became painters, jewelers, photographers, sculptors, and art critics. The plastic arts became inseparable companions in the development of revolutionary literary ventures, the nature of which, Martí, a pioneering writer, touched upon in 1875 in an essay on the Spanish poet and dramatist José Echegaray. At the conclusion of the essay, which is fundamentally a review of one of Echegaray's plays that Martí saw performed in Mexico City, Martí drifts into an enunciation of a series of linkages between artists and writers. All of which subsequently leads him to establish metaphoric, impressionistic, and even philosophic connections inspired by the canvases of painters the Cuban had studied early in the development of his modernist stylistic innovations. "In literature as in painting," he wrote, "there are so-called momentous styles":

Shakespeare makes me think of Rubens. Although he makes me think more of Michelangelo. Rubens displays enormous deformities, but always those of a deformed giant. Michelangelo dreams of robust trunks, huge muscles, dense atmospheric shadows, sinewy monsters in the gloom. Michelangelo had a touch of genesis and apocalypse. With this somber, daring form, he offers us an idea of the supreme slavery in which, with a capacity for total encompassment, everything flees, everything escapes, everything is repressed, is frightened and maddened.

(En literatura como en pintura, hay lo que se llama grandes maneras. Shakespeare me hace pensar en Rubens. Aunque más me hace pensar en Miguel Angel. Rubens tiene deformidades de gigante, pero es siempre un gigante deforme. Miguel Angel sueña troncos robustos, músculos rudos, apretadas tinieblas en la atmósfera y monstruos nervudos en las tinieblas. Había en Miguel Angel algo de génesis y apocalipsis. . . . Da, con este sombrío atrevimiento de la forma, idea de esta suprema esclavitud en que, con facultades para concebirlo todo, todo huye, todo se escapa, todo reprime, espanta, y enloquece.) (1963–1973, 15: 79–80)

In expanding the frontiers of literary language not just Martí but other writers associated with the modernist revolution were inspired by the visual arts and inserted the techniques of these arts in their texts. And, in addition, they tried their hand at art criticism as we shall see in the sections of this chapter.

JOSÉ MARTÍ: EUROPEAN, AMERICAN, AND MEXICAN ART

Martí's interest in the plastic arts and its relation to "painting with words" began in Cuba prior to the colonial government's order that he be deported to Spain.[1] We know, for example, that he studied drawing at the Academia de San Alejandro in Havana. But it was in Spain where he first developed his skills as an art critic. The Prado Museum, the Academy of San Fernando, as well as the galleries of Zaragoza sharpened his critical eye and in the late seventies generated a series of notes (1879) on several Spanish painters, including Francisco de Goya[2] and Raimundo de Madrazo.[3] However, it was his residency in the United States (1880–1895) that provided him with the opportunity to study the canvases of Western painters with an intensity that neither his stay in Europe, Mexico, Venezuela, or Guatemala afforded him. And it is in his essays written in the United States that we find theoretical notes of substance with respect to the nature of the visual arts. In 1885, for example, conjoining the sister arts of literature and painting, he wrote:

> Art like literature can neither be improvised nor transplanted: nor transplanted bear good fruit. To be powerful you must be genuine. In painting as in writing, only what is direct lasts. Art like fruit must mature on the vine. It is produced very slowly by means of the tenacious and indissoluble grouping of autochthonous defined elements that given the special characteristics of nature or the condensed and resistant products of particular spiritual movements, at the conclusion of long life, constitute the national character which like the soul reflected in facial features is mirrored in Art and Literature.

> (El Arte, como la Literatura, ni se improvisa ni trasplanta: ni trasplantado, da buen fruto. Para ser poderoso, ha de ser genuino. En pintura, como en letras sólo perdura lo directo. El Arte ha de madurar en el árbol, como la fruta. Se va haciendo despaciosísimamente, mediante la agrupación tenaz e indisoluble de los elementos nativos y distintos que, por los caracteres peculiares de la naturaleza o los productos condensados y resistentes de especiales direcciones del espíritu, constitutyen al fin de la larga vida el carácter nacional, que, como se sale el alma al rostro, en el Arte y en la Literatura se reflejan.) (1963–1973, 10: 228–29)

Martí wrote at first about Spanish painting. For him Goya was a revolutionary painter (15: 133), an innovative artist who inspired and moved the Cuban to transtextualize his paintings, many of which early in his role as an art critic he admired in Spain and later, from 1880 forward, he viewed in the galleries and museums of New York. Writing in Spain he opened his notes on Goya with an enraptured emotional "avant la lettre" discourse both impressionistic and pointillistic in style. When we read these notes at the outset, we have no idea which Goya painting has moved him. The reader needs to reach the end of the first sentence to discover it is *The Clothed Maja* whose legs remind him of a Titian canvas. It is significant that to describe the Maja the Cuban chose the Venetian master for his base of comparison since Titian achieved movement through his use of color and unity through "chromatic balance." Similarly, Martí, in his notes on the Maja focuses on specific chromatics—black eyes, flushed cheeks, red mouth:

> Never [he wrote] did the black eyes of a woman, nor the flushed cheeks, nor the Moorish eyebrow, nor the tiny red, thin mouth,—nor the torpid laxity, nor however beautiful and seductive the sinful thought of Andalusian love, [nor] anything that attempts to reveal it outwardly, or blemish it—[never] did they find a richer expression than in "La Maja." She's not thinking of a man; she is dreaming. Did Goya, he who overcame all sorts of difficulties,—by chance wish to dress the Venus, in order to give her an Andalusian touch, a heightened human quality, a certain palpable feminine essence?

> (Nunca negros ojos de mujer, ni encendida mejilla, ni morisca ceja, ni breve, afilada y roja boca,—ni lánguida pereza, ni cuanto de bello y deleitoso el pecaminoso pensamiento del amor andaluz, sin nada que pretenda revelarlo exteriormente, ni lo afee,—halló expresión más rica que en "La Maja." No piensa en un hombre; sueña. ¿Quiso acaso, Goya, vencedor de toda dificultad,—vestir a Venus, darle matiz andaluz, realce humano, existencia femenil, palpable, cierta?) (1963–1973, 15: 131)

Martí was entranced, visibly overwhelmed, by the beauty, mystery, voluptuousness, eroticism, and color of the portrait. For him Goya was a trailblazer who broke with all notions of conventionality in this painting. And though he found the clothed Maja more voluptuous than erotic, it is the covering of the body as in Casal's "Salomé" that heightens his sensuality and causes him to fantasize that were she to rise from her pillows and approach him with a kiss it would be the most natural thing in the world. But alas, he concludes, "She looks at no one!" (¡Pero no mira a nadie!) (1963–1973, 15: 131). The naked Maja interested him less. His critical eye focused briefly on her breasts, which led him to quote Baudelaire's observation that they appeared to have been created with a strabismic eye. Ah!, noted Martí, in response, Baudelaire wrote poetry as if, with a steady hand, he was carving white marble (15: 136)—an observation generated by the hybridity of form typical of Martí's discourse, which like Baudelaire's constantly incorporated the techniques of the sister arts in an effort to expand the limits of literary language.

Subsequent to these and other early notes, the impact of Goya's art on Martí never waned in its intensity. In February of 1888 in a letter to his Uruguayan friend, Enrique Estrázulas, on the subject of painting, he wrote that he cannot get Goya's *Maja* "out of his heart." Goya, he wrote, was a master, "one of the few major painters" ([uno] de los pocos pintores padres) (20: 189).

In New York—1880–1895—he continued to visit galleries. Shortly after his arrival in the United States *The Hour*,[4] a New York periodical devoted to the arts, invited him, through the intervention of a friend, Enrique Collazo, to review the latest museum and gallery exhibits. Martí was delighted but apprehensive because his English, though fairly good, was not polished enough for a sophisticated New York art journal. Among the many notes he left us about his initiation as a New York art critic, the following described his joy at accepting *The Hour*'s commission, but more importantly, it reveals his love for the plastic arts as well as his capacity for appreciating the creative spirit and aesthetic qualities of a host of major Renaissance and nineteenth-century artists:

> I have an unwavering love for art. Today I had a dollar and I spent it on Japanese cups; my wife is coming. I've uncovered the mysteries of color, I've grasped the chisel's secrets in marble pieces; a beautiful work of art is like a sister to me, *a blaze of color*, for me, a clear revelation of the thoughts and ideas that stirred the soul of the painter. In the Louvre I've felt something stir my soul standing before Murillo's pale shades. I've felt tears of gratitude for the palliate I've experienced contemplating the sketch of Fortuny's "Battle of Wad-Ras." Timidly I've moved my finger over the canvas of the Mexican Rebull to see if his steel blue was the canvas or a cloud. I've dialogued with Goya's "La Maja." I've had long conversations with Titian's Venuses. I've brought one home, and we live chastely in delicious company.

> (Yo amo tenazmente el arte. Hoy tenía un peso, y lo he gastado en tazas del Japón; mi mujer viene. He penetrado los misterios del color, he sorprendido en la obra del mármol los secretos del cincel; una obra bella es para mí una hermana, *un golpe de color*, para mí revelación clarísima de los pensamientos e ideas que agitaban el alma del pintor. He sentido dentro de mi alma frotarme algo, en el Louvre, ante los medios tintes de Murillo.

> Las lágrimas agradecidas, por el bien que de la contemplación
> de la obra recibía, se me han saltado de los ojos ante el boceto de
> "La batalla de Wad-Ras" de Fortuny. He hundido tímidamente
> el dedo en un lienzo del mexicano Rebull para convencerme
> de si aquel acerado azul era lienzo o nube. He hablado a solas
> con "La Maja" de Goya. He tenido largas pláticas con las Venus
> del Ticiano. Me ha traído una a casa, y vivimos castamente en
> deleitosa compañía.) (15: 285; emphasis mine)

Martí's notion of the personal registers of a painting's essence is expressed in his notes via the familial metaphor "sister" and is tied to his theory of modern art formulated in his essay on Juan Pérez Bonalde, "El Prólogo al poema del Niágara" (Prologue to the poem Niagara) in which he conceived modern art as a dynamic process of externalizing internal visions—a concept as well as a technique he incorporated into his own symbolic, metaphoric prose and the poems of his first book of verses, *Ismaelillo*. His chromatic image "blaze of color" constitutes an aesthetic affirmation of the Cuban's insistence upon the new perceptions of nature ushered in by modernity, and finally, "the thoughts and ideas" are related to Martí's notion of an emancipatory project initiated in the period of the Enlightenment but fundamental to the symbolic productions of modern sociocultural life whose precise features Martí confessed he could not yet see with absolute clarity. But in the contemplation of the paintings of the masters he was less ambiguous; in them he discovered the shortest path to uncovering truth (De Juan 1997, 11) and an instrumentality, related to the "thoughts and ideas," which he believed would move humanity toward the amelioration of the problems and pains of society (De Juan 1997, 12).

Martí's abundant texts on painting constitute an affirmation that the aesthetic gaze, fundamental to the notion of "painting modernism," was never absent from his purview. In 1889 he wrote his friend, Miguel Tedín: "You love painting as I do; each month I give myself a day of paintings so that romance and color fill my soul" (A Vd. le gustan los cuadros, como a mí, que me doy un día de cuadros cada mes, para que me entre el alma en romance y color) (7: 396).[5] And beginning with his stay in Mexico (1875) he developed an amazingly mature series of ideas on the nature of painting in the modern world.

> Innovation in painting should not cause utter falsity of color,
> faulty design, rigid vestments, lack of facial expression, and the

attractive placement of figures. . . . a painter who wishes to be more than a portraitist should learn to paint the wealth, movement, clashes and contrasts of color.

(La novedad en la pintura no debe llegar nunca a la completa falsedad de color, a la incorreción del dibujo, a la dureza de las ropas, a la carencia de expressión en las fisonomías y de gracia en la colocación de las figuras. . . . el pintor que quiere ser algo más que retratista, debe acostumbrar su pincel a las riquezas, movilidad, golpes luminosos y contrastes del color.)

. . . . . .

Art is a form of harmony. Sometimes irregularity is artistic; but asymmetry in painting should have its logic amid its disorders, just as the caprices of poetic fantasy should be consistent and grouped with unity. Monotony is dangerous for it extinguishes everything, just as it eradicates the sanctity and customs of love; in painting, parallel lines, symmetrical points, alternating and equal lines, geometrize figures, drain the composition, destroy the charm and movement of the work with the stiffness of straight lines. There is no beauty in rigidity; life is mutable, fluid, fleeting, malleable, active. . . . It should not be said of a painter that he is correct, it should be said that he is magnificent, innovative, inventive and impressive.

(El arte es una forma de la armonía. A veces, es artística la irregularidad; pero esta irregularidad en la pintura, debe ser lógica entre sus accidentes, como deben ser consecuentes y agrupados en unidad los caprichos de la fantasía poética. La monotonía es fiera porque lo extingue todo, como que hasta extingue las santidades y costumbres del amor; en pintura, las líneas paralelas, los puntos simétricos, las líneas iguales y alternas, geometrizan la figura, vacían el conjunto, destruyen con la dureza de las rectas, la gracia y las ondulaciones de la obra. No hay belleza en la rigidez; la vida es móvil, desenvuelta, abandonada, muelle, activa. . . . No debe decirse de un pintor que es correcto, debe decirse que es soberbio, innovador, brioso y grande.) (Martí 1961, 275–276).

The importance of Spain in the development of Martí's love for painting and his subsequent transfer of painterly techniques to his writing cannot be overstated. He first resided in Spain as an exile from 1871 to 1874, and in a second exile he visited briefly from October to December 1879. While there he familiarized himself with the most outstanding artists of the time, but especially with the production of two painters whose work he considered decisive in the formation of "modern art": Goya and Velázquez. And later, in New York, in an essay (1886) on the French impressionists and the modern Spanish painters he insisted that modern art stemmed from the innovations of the two Spanish giants—Velázquez and Goya:

> Velázquez resuscitated the forgotten people; Goya, who as a child sketched with all the sweetness of a Raphael, descended, wrapped in a *dark* cape, to the entrails of humanity, and with its *colors* described his trip upon his return—Velázquez was the naturalist: Goya the impressionist . . .

> (De Velázquez y Goya vienen todos,—esos dos españoles gigantescsos: Velázquez creó de nuevo los hombres olvidados; Goya, que dibujaba cuando niño con toda la dulcedumbre de Rafael, bajó envuelto en una capa oscura a las entrañas del ser humano y con los colores de ellas contó el viaje a su vuelta.—Velázquez fue el naturalista: Goya fue el impresionista.) (19: 304–305; emphasis mine)

Martí reviewed the work of some thirty-three Spanish painters (De Juan 1997, 42), but curiously, in spite of his admiration for Velázquez's painting, he never devoted an essay to his art. As for Goya, there is no organic essay either, but in a notebook, as we've already indicated, he left a significant series of commentaries that illuminate Goya's painting but, more importantly, shed light on Martí's revolutionary, entirely modern aesthetic theories. Of Goya's *La casa de los locos* (The insane asylum) he wrote:

> This canvas is a historical page [but also] a great poetic page. In this painting more than its form what amazes us is the artist's intrepid disregard of it. Genius embellishes the mistakes it creates, *especially those created consciously,* which enhance the

intent when so created. Genius embellishes the monsters it creates!

(Ese lienzo es una página histórica y una gran página poética. Aquí más que la forma sorprende el atrevimiento de haberla desdeñado. El genio embellece las incorreciones en que incurre, sobre todo voluntariamente, y para mayor grandeza del propósito, incurre en ellas. ¡El genio embellece los monstrous que crea!) (15: 132; emphasis mine)

Martí, ever the revolutionary modernist, celebrates Goya's daring rather than his conformity, specifically, his departure from sacrosanct academic norms, a principle that in his opinion enhances creativity. But the hand of the revolutionary, preoccupied with historical transformation and ideological change, counterbalances artistic innovation with a concern for historical evolution. This struggle of dualities is evident in his examination of Goya's *Corrida de toros en un pueblo* (Bull fight in a small town): in discussing the interplay of aesthetic and ideological values he attributes the greater importance to the latter. And he challenges academic and impressionistic painters, many blinded by contemporary chromatic experimentations,[6] to abandon affectations and, following Goya's example, to strive to achieve a powerful and useful expression superior to the vagaries of color (15: 132–133).

It should be understood that Martí always valued as fundamental the aesthetic qualities of a painting, a principle evident in his notes on Goya, which often reflect a transfer of French impressionistic styles. But, in spite of his appreciation of the more formal—including vanguard—artistic elements of a canvas, he considered a work of art deficient if it did not embrace what he termed a fundamental "idea." An artist—he insisted—as in the case of Goya—must be enamored of the importance of an idea, and at the same time, a revolutionary, a philosopher, a creator who reaches for new horizons and simultaneously demolishes all that smacks of terrible infamy (15: 133, 136).

Madrazo and Fortuny were also major Spanish painters for Martí, and what he learned from their work and Goya's is reflected in the painterly aspects of his prose and poetry. The Cuban included Madrazo in 1879 notes written in French, but his more significant commentaries belong to his New York period, 1880–1895. These critiques reflect two major influences: 1) Martí's familiarity with French impressionist paintings, first in

Paris and later, in New York art galleries; and 2) the process of modernization that Martí witnessed in the United States with both admiration and apprehension contrasted with the more relaxed and traditional mores of precapitalistic society of the countries south of the border in which he lived prior to establishing his residence in New York.

At the beginning of his essay on Madrazo (published in *The Hour*), Martí noted that the Spanish painter "discovered the secret of originality, not from the absurd fantasies of the Impressionist School nor from the disciples of Ultrarealism whose members [he wrote] desperately court the accolades of the critics" (ha encontrado el secreto de la originalidad, no en las absurdas fantasías de la escuela impresionista ni entre los discípulos del ultrarrealismo, ambas buscadoras desesperadas de críticas favorables) (15: 154). It should be noted that Martí harbored ambivalent feelings with respect to some of the impressionist experiments. But he admired the originality of their daring techniques involving color and light. And in connection with his critiques of old masters of Spanish painting— Madrazo or Goya—his essays reveal the influence of the impressionists on his style and his ideas. With his usual visionary perspicacity and "avant la lettre" appreciation, he connected the work of the impressionists with incipient art movements generated by the swell of economic and social transformations of industrializing nations, a process the Cuban was able to view over a span of fifteen years in New York. He wrote that the impressionists were painters who joined the ranks of artists in an era without altars, creators who neither have faith in what they do nor see or suffer the pain of having lost their faith. And lacking solid beliefs for which they might fight, he posited that on their canvases they hope to capture things that appear in life with enhanced beauty (19: 305). And as if the writer suddenly were transformed into a painter, Martí with broad and daring brushstrokes describes the works of the impressionists displayed in a New York gallery in 1886:

> They [the canvases] seem to be clouds dressed in their Sunday best: *some, completely blue; others all violet; there are yellowish seas; there are purple men; there is a green family.* Some canvases overwhelm us immediately. Others, at first glance tempt us to plunge our fist in them; [but] on second thought to take our hat off to the painter's daring; and, finally, to caress tenderly he who fought in vain to pour out on the canvas the profound distances and tenuous impalpable qualities with which vaporous light softens chromatic intensity.

(Parecen nubes vestidas de domingo: unas, todas azules; otras, todas violetas; *hay mares cremas; hay hombres morados; hay una familia verde.* Algunos lienzos subyugan al instante. Otros, a la primera ojeada, dan deseos de hundirlos de un buen puñetazo; a la segunda, de saludar con respeto al pintor que osó tanto; a la tercera, de acariciar con ternura al que luchó en vano por vaciar en el lienzo las hondas distancias y tenuidades impalpables con que suaviza el vapor de la luz la intensidad de los colores.) (19: 304; emphasis mine)

The critic's verbal palette matches that of the exhibited canvases. He describes chromatically: "Rivers of green, plains of red, mountains of yellow: as a group that's how the canvases of these mad new artists seem" (Ríos de verde, llanos de rojo, cerros de amarillo: esos parecen, vistos en montón, los lienzos locos de estos pintores nuevos) (15: 304). But as important as the chromatic transcriptions is the incorporation of painterly concepts in metaphorical constructs, or simply stated, the transfer of plastic techniques to modernist verbalizations. Writing to José Joaquín Palma, Martí turns to Raphael's art in order to describe Palma's verses: "You have more of Raphael's blues than of Goya's blacks" (Tu tienes más del azul de Rafael que del negro de Goya) (5: 94).

We stated earlier that Martí's concept of the impressionists' innovations was ambivalent. On the one hand he was dazzled by their chromatic experiments, but he questioned the intentionality of their work and, in some cases, the message or its absence. He wondered, furthermore, if they were aspiring to create the impossible by attempting a portrayal of nature at variance with what he called its fundamental constitution. As he put it:

They wish to copy reality, not as it is by virtue of its constitution, and how we see it in our mind, but as it appears in a transitory moment with the capricious effects of the play of light. They wish, given the soul's implacable thirst, [to achieve] the new and the impossible. They wish to paint as the sun paints and they fail.

(Quieren copiar las cosas, no como son en sí por su constitución y se las ve en la mente, sino como en una hora transitoria las pone con efectos caprichosos la caricia de la luz. Quieren, por la implacable sed del alma lo nuevo y lo imposible. Quieren pintar como el sol pinta, y caen.) (19: 305)

But, on the other hand, he noted that there was a message in the work of the impressionists that ought to not be overlooked. And its presence prompted him to theorize that their canvases reflected an angelic force that led them as artists connected to contemporary movements of change to create works that demonstrated a sympathy for truth in tandem with the stages of socioeconomic modernization. Thus, they painted the misery in which the humble live, the hungry dancers, the drunken workers, the withered peasant mothers, the perverted children of the damned, and so many swollen, odious, brutal portraits identified with the transformations that accompanied the new economic order of industrializing nations (19: 305–306). But what Martí considered the dark side of impressionist art was counterbalanced by the Cuban's final remarks on exiting the gallery where the impressionists were on display: the art of Manet, Renoir, and Pissarro, he concluded, made up for any and all deficiencies in drawing, violent landscapes, or the excessive reliance on Oriental perspectives (19: 306).

One of Martí's longest and most extraordinary critical essays on nineteenth-century artists is the 1889 review of Vasily Vereshchagin's art viewed in New York.[7] It is extraordinary for two reasons: 1) the discourse of the essay is infused with chromatic features, reflecting the Cuban's constant and highly artistic transfers of painting techniques to his literary style, and 2) it is an essay that constitutes a philosophical meditation on the nature of art and its relationship to social issues. From the very first paragraph of this ten-page essay the language is suffused with color: "Paris welcomed him [Vereshchagin] for his color . . ." (Por su color lo saludó París) (15: 429); "that's painting as it should be, painting with the light of the sun, without the quirkery of shadows and varnish! . . . That's fresh color, color without the blaze of truth, the dry color of objects in the light of day, not that of the academies, rhetorical and cloying!" (¡Esa es la pintura deseada, la pintura al sol, sin ardides de sombra y de barniz! . . . ¡Es el color fresco, el color sin brillo de la verdad, el color seco de los objetos al aire libre, y no eso de academias, retórico y meloso!) (15: 430). Or, from among the many touches of color in this essay, the following description whose metaphors are expressionistic and entwined in a synaesthetic relationship with the sound of music and the silence of evening color:

> And they say that these *somber, radiant,* unpolished, livid, *yellow* canvases, *painted with milk, painted with blood,* stand out, resplendent and huge, in comparison with the bland and discreet tapestries, among whose deep folds, birds seeking refuge, chirp musical notes plaintively. [They are] much like a cur-

tain that is opened, a curtain of *silent evening color*, which in its
crevices of blinding snow reveals the caverns of the Caucuses.

(Y dicen que esos cuadros sombríos, fúlgidos, crudos, lívidos,
amarillos, pintados con leche, pintados con sangre, se desta-
can, radiantes y enormes, de entre tapices blandos y discretos,
por entre cuyos profundos pliegues, como pájaros que buscan
asilo, se extiguen, trinando querellosas, las notas de la música.
¡Como un telón que se descorre, un telón del *color silencioso* del
anochecer, que revela con sus grietas de nieve deslumbradora,
los antros del Cáucaso.) (15: 429–430)

But color alone never satisfied the Cuban writer. He found in Vereshchagin's art the same shortcoming he perceived in those of many of his
contemporaries—the constant excess of emphasis upon expression to the
detriment of the faculty of creation, an overwhelming concern for the use
of chromatics instead of the creation of subjects worthy of coloration or,
as he put it:

the rendering of externals that only requires the eye of the
observer, rather than paintings in which the externals are used
in states and forms that produce an intimate caress, a mix of
submission and pride, in which human beings in the presence
of beauty, whether animate or inert, recognize and esteem
themselves . . .

(de la pintura de lo exterior, que sólo exige ojo para observar,
juicio para elegir, gracia para agrupar color, para reproducir,
sobre aquella otra pintura en que lo exterior se usa verazmente
en estado y formas que produzcan aquella caricia íntima, mezcla de sumisión y orgullo, con que el hombre en presencia de la
beldad, animada o inerte, se reconoce y estima . . .) (15: 432)

As for the art of the United States, Martí was not an admirer.[8] He
felt that the emphasis upon the acquisition of material wealth that he
observed all around him in U.S. society was not a stimulant to the creation
of major works of art. In an essay written in English about the fifty-fifth
exhibition of the National Academy of Design, we read: "Unfortunately, we cannot as yet consider the general spirit of the American school
of painting, because there is no school here. To copy nature, to imitate

European masters, to *give color* to caricatures, is not to create a school" (13: 469; emphasis mine). It is interesting that in enumerating the qualities he observed in the painting of Winslow Homer, Eastman Johnson, Arthur Quartley, Moran, Porter, Brown, or Gifford, he zeroed in on color, as he did in judging the art of important European painters.

However, in his art criticism, as in all other aspects of his writing, Martí was an evolutionist—that is, he constantly reconsidered and reevaluated.[9] And thus, eight years after his essay on the painting exhibited at the National Academy of Design, he wrote with a bit more, yet still constrained, enthusiasm about American art. He noted at the outset of his 1888 essay sent to *La Nación* that a few years prior it was sad to see the quality of U.S. painting exhibited in New York. American artists in his view followed English landscape painting and their seascapes were dark and crude; they lacked the charm and the crystalline quality of the sea; they were hard, pasty and "livid like meat about to spoil" (violáceas, como la carne que va para podre) (13: 479). But now, in the watercolors of this new exhibit, he discovered with pleasure elements of light and color in the canvases of the young artists of "this crude country" (este pueblo burdo) (13: 481).[10]

Martí's notion of the world embraced Latin America, Europe, the United States, and the Near and Far East. But his visioning of the art of his time, which he chronicled in notes, poems, and essays from 1875 to 1894 (De Juan 1997, 10), emphasized the art of the United States and Europe. He was very much aware of the history and culture of the Orient (see chapter 4), but he was less an Orientalist than Julián del Casal. Nevertheless he was familiar with the Japanese art that influenced European painters of his time and ultimately reached Latin America via European exports. But there are no major essays on Japanese painters or printmakers of his time. His intellectual curiosity, however, was incredibly broad, and in his complete works he provides random translations and notes on Em. Bergerat's work, *Les chefs d'oeuvres de l'art a l'exp. Univ. de 1878*,[11] a fragmentary essay which documents the development of Japanese art from its earliest periods to the nineteenth century.

DARÍO: EUROPE, JAPAN, AND LATIN AMERICA

It can be said, without exaggeration, that all of the Latin American modernists were attracted to the plastic arts. But rare are the examples of writers who also were consummate art critics such as Martí. Nevertheless, many of Darío's texts, prose and poetry, reveal a rich palette of colors, and his writing exhibits the fine line of an observant artist in the plastic sense of the word. The Nicaraguan was fascinated by the newly developed late nineteenth-century techniques in photography as well as other related forms of art (re)production, subjects that he included in his essay on Adolphe Goupil (1806–1893),[12] subtitled "El tesoro de Bellas Artes Modernas" (An album of fine art). Darío was particularly grateful to Goupil because, as he notes in his essay (1: 632), the album made available to Latin American countries reproductions of paintings and sculpture that, as noted previously,[13] allowed modernist writers to view emerging European experimental, vanguard art forms and transfer their techniques to their prose and poetry. Goupil's collection of reproductions was, to be sure, but one of many sources of industrial and photographic images that late in the nineteenth century inspired modernists in their search for a new creative lexicon capable of giving voice to their angst in the face of social and economic transformations that redefined their role within society.

Darío's writing reflected the emancipatory struggle of late nineteenth-century modernists and spoke of the process in the prologues to his major books of poetry[14] without developing a meditative instrument comparable to Martí's philosophic, social, and historical awareness of the nature of the effect of modernization on the status of art and the altered role of the artist.[15] As Angel Rama noted so incisively, Darío was thrown into the "marketplace" of Latin American industrializing communities in the latter half of the nineteenth century (Rama 1967). However, there is no doubt that Darío understood the significance as well as the consequences of the process of modernization. He also was well aware of the nature of modernity's manufacturing innovations, its scientific and technical advances that ushered in photography and other forms of art reproduction:

> Goupil [he wrote] places at his service the light of the sun, industry and artist: photography, etchings, prints, photoengravings, everything is included in his development plans. . . . Large-scale canvases, cartoons for large frames, special albums and notebooks, everything has been made available by his workshops for collectors, aficionados and art lovers.

> (Goupil pone a su servicio el rayo del sol, el industrial y el artista: fotografía, agua fuerte, grabado, fotograbado, todo entra en su programa de desarrollo. . . . Cuadros de gran tamaño,

cartones para anchos marcos, albums y cuadernos especiales, todo ha sido por sus talleres difundido para coleccionistas, aficionados y amigos del arte.) (1: 635)

Fascinated with this new industrial tool, the enthused Darío provides a transposition of a bullfight scene by Alejandro Wágner,[17] which Goupil and his associate Gebbie included in their collection of art reproductions. It is a transposition rich in chromatics, one that comes close to the painterly techniques of Martí's art criticism:

> The *delicate coloring* distinguishes his work. The *dark shading* of the bull in the center of the painting and the *white horse* at its side create an excellent effect; the grouping of the spectators, the other body in the arena, the clothing and the archeological elements constitute a truly pictorial reconstruction.

> (La tinta fina hace su obra. La mancha negra del toro en el centro del cuadro y el caballo blanco que está a su lado, son de un buen efecto; la agrupación de concurrencia, la otra figura que está en la arena, la parte indumentaria y arqueológica, son una verdadera reconstrucción pictórica.) (1: 636)

Darío is an enthusiastic and knowledgeable critic. It is clear from the material included in this essay that he is familiar with contemporary artists—French, Spanish, and American. In his commentaries on their work, he includes biographical and historical information about painters, some obscure today, such as Luis Ricardo Falero, Jean Ferdinand Monchablon, or Emile Auguste Carolus-Durán. However, he is also a champion of Latin American art whose influence among the modernists is significantly less important than that of the European or Japanese artists of the period. Darío, in his essay on Alfredo Ramos Martínez, quotes some of the Mexican painter's ideas on the ideological nature of late nineteenth-century society, which he characterizes, in the fashion of Marinetti, as a time of "electricity," of instantaneous mobility for the painter, the sculptor, and the poet (1: 659). Darío, with his constant visioning of the significance of the past for the present, views Martínez's work in the light of Titian's and notes that had he lived in the days of the "magical" Venice and been a member of Titian's salon he would have "created melodies of light, songs of color, poetic watercolors . . . (compuesto melodías de luz, cantos de color, poémi-

cas acuarelas . . .) (1: 659). But as an afterthought Darío, reflecting arche-
typical modernist despondency, concludes that in spite of some spiritual
atavistic qualities he senses in Ramos Martínez, he lacks qualities that come
from periods of history that are more beautiful, more noble more disposed
to thinking and feeling. Unfortunately, he writes, the Mexican artist lives
in a "dry period" (1: 660), the period of Latin American modernization.

Darío, like many Latin American modernists, understood the relationship of painting to writing. In his essay on the Mexican artist Ramos Martínez, he noted that "there is a great deal of painting in poetry and much
poetry in painting" (Hay mucho de pintura en la poesía, y hay mucho de
poesía en la pintura . . .) (1: 661). Darío illustrated this theoretical statement with Martínez's art: he paints poetry, creating in painting what Grieg
achieved in music; he refrains from copying, unlike the many "photographic" artists who earn medals in the salons (1: 662). His illusions, wrote Darío,
are blue and the compositions of his painting are chromatic, for which reason the Nicaraguan considered him to be a true painter in the tradition of
Velázquez and Rembrandt (es un puro pintor de la tradición de velasquina-
rembrandesca) (1: 663). This coupling of painting and writing is also evident in the essay on two French military painters ("Pintores de batallas"
[Painters of battles]) (1: 725–729)—Edouard Détaille and Alphonse Marie
de Neuville. Not only does Darío have a thorough knowledge of their canvases, which he describes with detailed transpositions, but at the conclusion
he links their art to Alphonse Daudet and Paul Déroulede: the paintings,
short stories, and poetry kindle passion for the beautiful and glorious nation
of France" (los cuadros, los cuentos y los versos encienden . . . el amor a su
bello y glorioso país de Francia) (1: 729).

Of all the essays written by Darío that deal with painting, none com-
pares in breadth of sophistication and knowledge of contemporary art than
"La labor de Vittorio Pica" (1: 761–188).[18] It is a lengthy prose piece that
to date has remained largely unstudied—as is the case of other Darió essays
and narratives. In the Pica essay the Nicaraguan speaks of his personal relationship with Vittorio Pica, his visit to his native Naples, and the two volumes of his criticism—with illustrations—which Darío examines and then
adds his own commentaries. His commentaries illustrate the depth of his
understanding and knowledge of the plastic arts. There is no doubt that "La
labor de Vittorio Pica" constitutes an important essay in its own right, but
it also stands as a documented source of Darío's revolutionary plastic and
visionary discourse steeped in styles and techniques of the sister arts that he
then transferred to literary discourse. Pica's reproductions of paintings run

the full gamut of nineteenth-century art, both European and Oriental. And the two volumes that Darío examines with excitement and enthusiasm confirm the fact, previously noted in the case of Casal's "Museo ideal," that the Latin American modernists by and large gleaned their knowledge of contemporary visual arts from reproductions rather than from the originals of canvases or sculptures. Martí, as we've indicated previously, is an exception, and it is conceivable that so was Tablada,[19] but most Latin American writers relied upon secondary, photographic images for their knowledge of contemporary plastic arts.

Darío's commentaries are encapsulated in short sections as he turns the pages of Pica's reproductions. The turning of the pages of Pica's work has a mobile quality suggestive of cinematic scenic successiveness: "He aquí primero los artistas macabros" (First we "see" the macabre artists) (1: 762). And then in the following paragraph he goes on to say that Henry de Groux comes next (viene después) (1: 763). In examining this essay it seems to us important to understand that its contents—in relation to Darío's painterly language and his storehouse of art history—is intertwined with his friend's broad knowledge of art. In short, we cannot assume all of Darío's critical commentaries are solely of his making. But, in the light of modernism's fundamental processing and retextualizing the Other and Others (i.e., cultures, historical periods, writing, painting, music, sculpture), melding concepts, ideas, or styles into new forms and formats, what we have in the case of the Darío-Pica coupling is a transposition of a storehouse of knowledge that is not disconnected from the transpositional representation and re-creation of canvases seen in museums or in photographic reproductions that we have already studied.

In this essay Darío's art criticism constitutes a duality that conjoins two streams of visualizations (his and Pica's) whose end result is the repainting of Western and Oriental art. This process is confirmed at the end of section 2 when the Nicaraguan reverts to the Pica text and we read in Italian Pica's commentary generated by the creations of the "macabre artists": "And the sun which has returned again . . . dispels all the frightening and cackling creatures of the imagination of Redon, Rops, di Groux and Goya" (E il sole, che é tornato di nuovo . . . discaccia tutte le panrose [*sic*] e ghignanti fantasime di Redon e di Rops, di Groux e di Goya) (1: 763).

In dealing with the Pica texts and its illustrations, Darío's language is eminently painterly. Thus, in section 2 of the essay, as he closes in upon a Goya "Caprichos" plate, visual language suggesting a virtual canvas overtakes critical commentary and we read:

The elegant, timid young woman is about to pull a tooth from the man just hung; . . . satire humanizes the ass and the monkey; the naked witches fly on their brooms. . . . But a ray of light penetrates the workplace in which the artist thumbs through his collections.

(La moza gallarda y miedosa va a arrancar al ahorcado un diente; . . . la sátira humaniza al asno al mono; desnudas van las hehiceras sobre el palo de escoba. . . . Mas un rayo de luz llega al gabinete de trabajo en que el artista hojea sus colecciones.) (1: 763)

There is a section devoted to Japanese art—Oriental canvases admired by many of the modernists who transferred Eastern artistic techniques into revolutionary and experimental Latin American literary styles. And if we follow Darío's thoughts as he thumbs the pages of Pica's work, in section 3 there is a description of the Kiyonaga canvases of movements, symbols, and reveries, of the art of Hokusai, Utamaro, and Yeisan. In subsequent sections, following Pica's ordering, and sometimes even including remarks of the Neapolitan critic—for example, "Pica says that Fernand Khno[p]ff[20] is a refined artist full of the most mysterious symbolic subtlety and admirably qualified to express it with a meticulous expert brush" (dice Pica que es Fernand Khno[p]ff refinado artista, lleno de la más misteriosa sutileza simbólica y admirablemente apto para expresarla con pincel minucioso sabio) (1: 772)—intermixed with his own comments: "Ruisoñol frequently spoke to me of Evenepoel who died young and would have been wonderful" (Muchas veces me ha hablado Ruisoñol de Evenepoel[21] que murió muy joven, y que habría sido glorioso) (1: 772). Then we come to a section on Aubrey Beardsley, admired by Darío for his black and white drawings and especially for his "figurative" commentaries of Oscar Wilde's *Salomé*. Here Darío waxes poetic and speaks of "an acute vice, eastern, deep-seated sin, lust that can only be understood in terms of erotic reveries" (vicio agudo, oriente, pecado inmenso, lujuria, tan solo comprensible por la lujuria de los ensueños eróticos) (1: 774). His comments on Beardsley's art and the quality of his experimentations go much beyond the English illustrator's art and reach into the aesthetic frame of mind of the modernist and contemporary world: "There is—writes Darío—a strange and mixed world in his art with disassociations that have the quality of hallucination and the specter of insubstantiality" (En él [Beardsley] hay un mundo extraño y revuelto en una disociación de cosas que tiene de la alucinación o de la aparición hipnagógica) (1: 774). Darío, who usually falls short in his essays of Martí's broad theoretical and/or philosophic vision, with comments such as these reveals a significant understanding of the disconnection and introspection of modernist Latin American culture and literature to whose revolutionary modes of expression the Nicaraguan was a major contributor.

In a subsequent section of Pica's anthology devoted to artists who portray scenes of war, Darío, like Martí, writes passionately of Goya's art. Both modernists were attracted to Goya's macabre scenes, which for both constituted a countercultural descent into the inner hidden recesses of human life, a glimpse of the underface of reality, in short an alternate universe whose "time out of joint" is characteristic of modernism's prose and poetry. For Darío the Spanish painter was

> the great Goya, who of war and its disasters left a macabre and horrible wealth of absolute, terrifying beauty. Who has not admired [he continued] the strength of expression and the extraordinary personality of the technique evident in the marauders who denude the dead, the horror of the fugitives, the fear of the victims, and the ferocity of the murderers, the violations, the horrible impaled victim, the flight in the face of the fire, the dead woman carried away together with the crying child, the panic of those who find themselves threatened by guns!

> (el gran Goya, que dejó de la guerra y sus desastres una mina macabra y horrible, de absoluta y terrífica belleza. ¡Quién no ha admirado la fuerza de expresión y la personalidad portentosa de la técnica en los merodeadores que desnudan a los muertos, en el horror de los fugitivos, en el espanto de las víctimas y la ferocidad de los matadores, en las violaciones, en el espantoso mutilado empalado, en la huída ante el incendio, en la muerta que conducen junto con la niña que llora, en el pavor de los que se ven amenazados por los fusiles!) (1: 778)

And finally, in the Pica essay, among so many other artists, special attention and commentary are given to artists of *eccezione*, such as James Ensor and Edvard Munch, painters of an alienated world who inspired Latin American modernists.

JOSÉ JUAN TABLADA: PARISIAN IMPRESSIONS

Paris was the cultural and artistic Mecca of the Latin American modernists. And although Tablada was drawn to the Orient and is best remembered for his "Orientalisms," he also was fascinated with the visual arts and the urban beauty of Paris. In his essay entitled "Orchids, Gastón La Touche,[22] Porcelains, and Prints" (Orquídeas, Gastón La Touche, Porcelanas y Estampas) (1988: 134–144), in the course of a five-hour stroll through Parisian neighborhoods, the Mexican modernist interrupts his walk because he spies two paintings in a vast store window. Through the medium of enthusiastic transpositions Tablada captures the chromatics and lines of the originals viewed through the storefront display:

> There are two canvases, each with a female figure amid strange shadows riddled with precious stones and dreamy light filtered through trees reminiscent of the *Thousand and One Nights*. The feeling of feminine charm reminds one of Watteau; but a Watteau who would have charged his palette with the colors of Venice and the scintillating quality of a Bagdad jeweler. An atmosphere of happy melancholy envelops the women who with affected XVIIIth century sensuality have the pomp and phantasmagoria of certain Poe heroines.
>
> (Son dos cuadros con sendas mujeres entre una extraña penumbra acribillada por la luz de ensueño y de pedrería que filtra a través de árboles de las *Mil y una noches*. El sentimiento de la gracia femenina recuerda Watteau; pero a un Watteau que hubiera llevado a su paleta el festival cromático de Venecia y la cintilación de un joyero de Bagdad. Atmósfera de dichosa melancolía envuelve a aquellas mujeres que tienen con remilgada sensualidd del siglo XVIII, el fausto y la fantasmagoría de ciertas heroinas de Edgar Poe.) (135)

It is especially interesting to note that at the conclusion of the description of one of the paintings in the window, Tablada connects La Touche's art with the work of a dreamer who searches the inner recesses of the (un)conscious, indicating a preference for the same variety of visualizations that captured Darío's imagination in his review of Pica's albums. Both canvases, he says, are "works of that sensual dreamer, the magnificent deluded [artist] who with Aladdin's lamp illuminates modern painting" (obras de ese soñador sensual, de ese magnífico alucinado que con una lámpara de Aladino ilumina la pintura moderna) (1988: 136).

In "Abdülhamit's Jewels" (Las Joyas de Abdülhamit) (1988: 157–160), Tablada's plastic visualization deals with a collection of jewels on view in a gallery that his prose then transforms via Parnassian enunciations into a chromatic painting:

> The *display*, indeed, is magnificent. . . . Over films which simulate astral clouds, over velvets black as the dreaded night, tiaras, crowns, headpieces and pectorals, necklaces and bracelets with settings that are a masterpiece of workmanship sparkle with magnificent jewels.

> (En efecto, el *display* es soberbio. . . . Sobre gasas que fingen nubes siderales, sobre terciopelos negros como el pavor nocturno, diademas y coronas, cascos y pectorals, collares y ajorcas hacen irradiar las piedras magníficas en montaduras que son obras maestras de artificio.) (157–158)

And upon exiting the gallery and traversing a bridge over the Seine, he paints the beauty of the scene before him:

> on traversing the Seine bridge, I saw a radiance in the pallid waves and I seemed to perceive the pale bodies of strangled odalisques floating adrift in the blood-red waters of the Bosphorus.

> (al pasar sobre un Puente del Sena, vi en las ondas lívidos fulgores y creí distinguir los pálidos cuerpos de las odaliscas enstranguladas flotando a la deriva sobre las sangrientas aguas del Bósforo.) (160)

And, finally, among Tablada's Parisian pages we note on more than one occasion his unwavering dedication to Oriental subjects:[23] for example, "The Yellow Watteau" (El Watteau Amarillo) in which he describes with passion an exhibit of Utamaro's work and decries Paris's superficial and sparse enthusiasm and understanding of Japanese art with the exception of the work of Hokusai and Utamaro (1971, 123–131).

6

AN EPILOGUE AND CONCLUSION

Words That Create Objects

In the preceding chapters we examined modalities of modernist writing during the period of its initial flowering up to the early twentieth century (1875–1920) and pointed out how Latin American literature during these years was influenced by the visual arts in a variety of formats. However, it is our contention, expressed in our recent research, that modernist literature continued to inspire writers beyond its initial periods of development and that the plastic arts also continued to leave their imprint on modern/contemporary Latin American letters.[1] To posit this chronological concept requires that we consider modernism's rise and subsequent development in terms of a broad cultural period with a multiplicity of evolving, varied styles, languages, and concepts. The Spanish writer Juan Ramón Jiménez years ago defended the notion of a modernist century, a notion not in conflict with other broad time frames such as the Western Renaissance or the Latin American colonial period, which embrace a galaxy of differing styles of writing.

In short, our contention is that modernism, conceived originally as a transnational literary and social manifestation connected to the Hispanic world of the nineteenth and early twentieth centuries is no longer a defensible theoretical position, chronologically or aesthetically. Revisionist critical studies in the past twenty years have demonstrated the importance of studying the ties between the diverse literary and social texts of the nineteenth century, during which modernism first appeared, and their subsequent transformations over time—from early modernist to vanguard literature forward—all of which mold cultural and artistic patterns of the postmodern Western world in which the power of the visual arts is linked to literary art.[2]

89

Modernist literature was generated by a long-standing universal crisis that dissolved traditional values and mores in the Western world, and, according to Federico de Onís, transformed art, science, religion, and politics as well as major aspects of life in general (176) over a broad time frame. If we accept this theoretical position presently held by major scholars, then modernism needs to be tied to modernity and envisioned as a protean process of liberation whose roots nourish the revolutionary ideas that first flowed from the Western Renaissance, especially the exploration of the spiritual spaces of individual existence as the center of the world in lieu of the spaces of a preordained and hierarchically structured universe. In short, modernism, marked by an anguished, persistent, and prolonged search of heretofore unknown regions of experience, rejects preordained ideas sanctioned by organized religions and protected by social practices and struggles to create counterhegemonic narrations whose enunciations abandon essentialism in favor of existentialism (see Jiménez 1962) and create the fragmented, chaotic, experimental art and literature that is also of our (post)modern world. There is, in short, a metafictive impulse inherent in contemporary letters that Linda Hutcheon describes as the persistence of the past in the interstices and intertexts of contemporary literary practice that scales the heights of new horizons and creates new styles and new languages. But, in our view there is also a second movement or impulse, one directed toward the cultural archive of the past, one that Georges Duby recognizes as an inheritance that every generation of writers embraces and reconstructs in a movement or impulse directed toward the future. To summarize, the experimentalism of modernist writing examined in the previous chapters constitutes a continuous search for new forms of art—even today—forms that reach into the past while proposing novel, ever-changing modes of expression.

In this chapter we hope to exemplify this concept by examining an aspect of the poetry of Vicente Huidobro, whose writing is rooted in modernism but at the same time transcends its traditional horizons by expanding the limits of verbal art through the incorporation of visual forms.[3] Huidobro's writing moves the word into spheres of visualization by transforming words into objects or into images that have double signification—as literary art and as plastic art. His revolutionary poetry is not disconnected from past performance;[4] the past in his writing is absorbed and/or retextualized to create novel enunciations. Cedomil Goic, one of Huidobro's major critics, unfortunately glosses over and underestimates the transfer and resurgence of the past in Huidobro's work when he writes, "there is a definite break with the previous Chilean poetry as well as with the principal influential European currents, namely modernism, and connected with it, French Parnassianism and symbolism" (hay sí una ruptura con la actitud poética inmediatamente anterior en la poesía chilena y con las principales corrientes europeas de influencia, cuales eran el *Modernismo* y, a través de él, el Viejo *Parnaso* y el *Simbolismo* francés) (61).

In Huidobro's experimentation with innovative forms of expression, contrary to Goic, we detect a *double* line of influence and continuity, past/present to future: 1) the transfer to a literary format of spatial techniques originally associated with the plastic arts, especially painting and sculpture, and 2) antecedents within Hispanic modernist poetry (overlooked by Goic), especially in the poetry of Rubén Darío and José Asunción Silva. To be more precise, Huidobro's poetic language, via a combinatory practice, assumes the substance and form of a line drawing, a sculpture, or a painting—especially Cubist; his word/objects have a sculptural form, a palpable visual form, and can even be viewed as architectural design.

The influence of painting in Huidobro's poetry is not surprising. During his stay in Paris prior to World War I he established friendships with a host of artists such as Jacques Lipchitz, Francis Picabia, Picasso, Juan Gris, and Max Ernst, to mention the most prominent. And he considered himself a Cubist in his early period of writing—1916–1917—when he was a major figure in the production of the French periodical *Nord-Sud*, which published calligrammes, that is, typographic spatiality and poems with blank spaces often without punctuation.[5]

It is the calligrammes that interest us in Huidobro's writing as we pursue the extension over time of modernist literature. And although the French influence, which is so pervasive in all of modernist art, was a major factor in the development of Huidobro's, there are, as we have suggested earlier, Hispanic antecedents that merit examination even if it is not clear they constitute a direct influential tie to Huidobro's experiments. Among Rubén Darío's early poetry, in his *Rimas*, for example, there is an experiment with metrics that timidly foreshadows later experiments such as Huidobro's. The lines are short; the poem is a nocturnal evocation of a dream related in a physically narrow typographical arrangement whose constructed form on the page conveys a syncopated rhythm of disjointed nocturnal visions replete with social, picaresque commentary—the product, says the poet, of his rattled nerves:

> One night
> I had a dream.

> Opaque moon,
> black sky,
> I was in a mournful
> Cemetery
> With shadows
> and silence.
> In shrouds
> Half bound,
> emaciated,
> skeletons
> very affable
> and content,
> received
> my visit
> . . . . . .
>
> (Una noche
> tuve un sueño.
> Luna opaca,
> cielo negro,
> yo en un triste
> cementerio
> con la sombra
> y el silencio
> En sudarios
> medio envueltos,
> descarnados
> esqueletos
> muy afables
> y contentos,
> mi visita
> recibieron.
> . . . . . .)
>   (*Rimas* 1887)[6]

Or, in José Asunción Silva's poetry the experimentations are metric, typographical, and visual but also based upon sound as in "Los maderos de San Juan" (The carpenters of San Juan), a poem in which there is a repeated refrain that simulates the sound of the saws:

¡Aserrín¡
¡Aserrín!
¡Aserrín!

Huidobro's experimentations go much further; they create a visual image, an object of recognizable form while at the same time preserving a traditional enunciation as in "Exprés":

London   Madrid   Paris
            Rome   Naples   Zurich
    Locomotives covered with algae
Whistle on the plains

            (Londres   Madrid   París
        Roma   Nápoles   Zurich
    Silban en los llanos
            Locomotoras cubiertas de algas)

The poet's message is both verbal and graphic. The cities of the poem are enumerated with spaces between and placed in line to simulate the cars of the express train. But, at the same time the words express a concept both concrete and visual. In short, the words are used by the poet to create objects; the palette is verbal and the end result is a spatial design that parallels the painter's use of line and color. In "Torre Eiffel" (Eiffel tower) the technique is similar. The tower is visualized as a "celestial guitar" (Guitarra del cielo); its structural reality is transferred typographically via a verbal arrangement. The tower is also perceived by the poet as a beehive of words or an inkwell of honey (Eres una colmena de Palabras / O un tintero lleno de miel). And the steps of the tower are "drawn" typographically as they might be in a painting:

        Do

                re

                        mi

                fa

                    sol

                        la

                            si

                                do
    Y ya estamos arriba (And we've reached the top)

To complete the visuals of the poem, we note that it was published in Madrid in 1918 together with one of Robert Delauny's[7] series of paintings of the Eiffel Tower—an artistic linkage that confirms the conjoining of painting and poetry.

The exploration of the plastic arts in the production of modernist writing has taken us through a multiplicity of forms. The persistent presence of the visual arts constitutes an expansion of the limits of literary arts, which is/was fundamental to the exploration of self and the creation of a new "self" in relation to the universe that constituted the fundamental element of early modernist writing. The complex process of social and cultural modernization with its melding of sister arts that began in the nineteenth century continued to generate new forms of literary expression in the twentieth century. The search for the "new" is not exhausted in our view; it is a project without end, an experimental process in which contemporary writers seek to transgress traditional boundaries of expression by visualizing novel painted, sculpted, or photographed universes. Our post- or post-post(modern) world is defined by its chaos, its disconnections and the cultural reactions to the fragmentation of traditional social mores. It is also defined by the retextualizion of the past and a search for the "new" that was the hallmark of modernist "vanguard" literature that has left a vital imprint upon today's art and literature.

NOTES

INTRODUCTION

1. We use the term *Latin American* throughout the chapters of this book even though we do not include Brazilian modernism, whose genesis and development, while not entirely distinct from that of Spanish America's, has enough inherent differences as well as a chronological development that would require a separate exploration.

2. A notion that was fundamental to José Martí's aesthetics, as we shall seeing in the narrative of the chapters that follow.

3. The two quoted concepts come from John Berger's book, *Ways of Seeing* (London: British Broadcasting Corporation, 1972), 7.

4. See, for example, Tinajero's affirmation in 2004 that "el modernismo hispanoamericano se sitúa aproximadamente entre 1888 y 1916" (1). For a revisionist, contemporary examination of the chronological limits of modernism and its aesthetic and social significance, see Schulman (2002).

5. For example, Schulman (2002, 1981, and 1987).

6. See Schulman (1986).

7. Another way of defining modernism is offered by Zavala: "Modernism is both a form of social organization (modernity) and a term of epochal diagnosis of the localized crises of the fundamental problems of technology and industrialization, of aesthetic experience and commodification" (109).

8. Martí (Cuba, 1853–1895) and Manuel Gutiérrez Nájera (Mexico, 1859–1895) are considered today the initiators of Latin American modernism in the Spanish language.

9. "El poema del Niágara," a prologue Martí wrote in 1882 for a lengthy poem by the Venezuelan Juan Antonio Pérez Bonalde. The translations of this and other Latin American texts, given the absence of published translations,

are mine. The Martí citations are from his complete works (*Obras completas*, 1963–1978).

10. The Darío citations are from the five-volume edition of his complete works (*Obras completas*), "Lo fatal" (5: 941) and "¡Ay, Triste . . ." (5: 921). In support of the interconnection of writers and painters belonging to the initial period of modernization, and responding to social practice, it is significant to note that Paul Gauguin has a very large canvas that has to be read from right to left—birth to death—entitled *Where do we come from? What are we? Where are we going?* (1897–1898).

11. See *Modernity and Modernism; French Painting in the Nineteenth Century*, 1.

12. A volume of poetry inspired by the musical antecedent of the Roman Catholic hymns of irregular meter sung before the Gospel and an example of modernism's search for self-definition by retextualizing past practices, literary and musical.

13. It should be noted that in Darío's vast writings there is an alternate discourse, one tied more closely to the realities of his period and one that at times reflects the search for Latin American cultural authenticity, liberation, and even anti-imperialism.

14. "Nuestra América." We have modified Esther Allen's otherwise excellent translation of Martí's *Selected Writings* (293).

15. See Paul Johnson, who dates the onset of modernity between 1815 and 1830 and includes among the signs of modernity the loss of Spain's colonies in the New World and the ensuing inception of chaos in Latin American social and economic history.

16. Ashcroft, Griffins, and Tiffen state there is a need to revise traditional lineal concepts of literary historiography, and they affirm in reexamining American literature that there exists a pattern that we consider applicable to Latin American literary history, that is, "a metonymic of a continual process of subversion and appropriation which predates the concerns of modernism and postmodernism and which may well be centered in their post-coloniality" (163).

17. See such major examples as Darío's "El rey burgués," Casal's "La sociedad de La Habana," or Martí's essays on life in the United States or his novel *Lucía Jerez*.

CHAPTER 1. CROSSING BOUNDARIES: THE SEARCH FOR A NEW DISCOURSE

1. The Oriental influences will be treated in a later chapter in which we examine the nature of Latin American modernist Orientalisms and the attraction of some of the modernists to the paintings of Hiroshige and Hokusai.

2. The gaze "may be characterized at once as a means of knowing and as a weapon of embodiment . . ." (Jacobs 1).

3. Curator notes to the Picasso exhibit at the Metropolitan Museum of Art, April 7, 2010–August 15, 2010.

4. Federico de Onís in his anthological history of Hispanic verse considers *Ismaelillo* the first truly modernist volume of poetry.

5. This organization of space is similar to but predates the spatial visualizations of symbolic expressionists such as Marc Chagall (1887–1985).

6. Although we do not know in which year Martí read Rimbaud, we do know he was inspired by his work in view of the fact that in a notebook entry dated 1894 he wrote: "*Rimbaud*, the author of the sonnet A noir, E blanc, I rouge, &" (64: 81).

7. All French eighteenth-century painters. Watteau was particularly popular with the modernists, and some like Darío dwelled on his relationship with Madame Pompadour. Darío in *Azul* . . . has a section entitled "Un retrato de Watteau" (A Watteau painting, 1950–1953,).

8. Horace's analysis of the relationship of painting and poetry in his *Ars poetica*. See also Lessing's eighteenth-century discussion in his *Laocoön*.

9. We use Krieger's definition: "Ekphrasis . . . clearly presupposes that one art . . . is defining its mission through its dependence on the mission of another art—painting, sculpture or others" (6).

10. Luis de Góngora (1561–1627), for example, during the Spanish Golden Age incorporated chromatic discursive elements in his poetry.

11. All citations referring to "En Chile" come from Alvaro Salvador's edition of Darío's *Azul*. . . .

12. The object of this representation is to overcome the limitation of words used to describe an object: spatial values are utilized to augment the impact of the temporal los valores espaciales se utilizan para aumentar el impacto del flujo temporal lingüístico.

13. With regard to Darío's rejection of bourgeois materialism in the short stories of *Azul* . . . , Lida notes that a distinguished historian of Latin American letters observes that these narratives chronicle the suffering and the dreams of a poor poet among the wealthy bourgeois (26n3).

14. Darío in his description of aspects of life in Valparaiso, Chile strikes an antimodern note. His enunciations are at variance with Marinetti's futuristic concept of rapid movement. In his later years, Darío expressed a somewhat dim view of Marinetti's futurism. But early on, in *Azul* . . . his antimodern note is expressed through a critique of modernity's rapid lifestyle: "Valparaiso transacts its business, walks like lightening, stocks its stores and invades banks, . . . and at night bustles about in its streets . . ." ("Valparaíso que hace transacciones, que anda a pie como una ráfaga, que puebla los almacenes e invade los bancos, . . . por la noche bulle en la calle . . ."] (125–126).

15. In November of 1888, in a letter to Pedro Nolasco Prendes, Darío wrote: "If I could create in verse José Martí's *luminous* grandeur! Or if Martí could transform his prose into verse!" (¡Si yo podría hacer verso las grandezas luminosas de José Martí! O si ¡Martí pudiera escribir su prosa en verso!) (2002, 99; emphasis mine).

16. Darío glossed over and failed to mention the enormous debt he owed to Martí's essays, which he read during his early Chilean period in Valparaíso.

CHAPTER 2. PAINTED NARRATIONS: THE MODERNIST NOVEL

1. The *crónica* is a Hispanic hybrid genre that can sometimes be compared to an essay, other times to a journalistic prose piece. The modernists cultivated the *crónica* and endowed it with artistic prose in the majority of cases.

2. For the best edition to date of this novel as well as an excellent introduction to it, see Belem Clark de Lara and Ana Elena Díaz Alejo's volume 11 of Manuel Gutiérrez Nájera's *Obras* (Mexico: Universidad Nacional Autónoma de México, 1994).

3. These novels frequently appeared in installments in newspapers and magazines, and it was sometimes more than a hundred years before all the pieces of the text were point. Nájera's, for example, first appeared in book form in 1994.

4. See González's selective study of modernist novels in which he observes that in these novels, "words resemble objects" (las palabras se semejan como cosas) (25).

5. See our discussion in chapter 4 of Julián del Casal's *Museo ideal* (Ideal museum). The sonnets of this section of his poems were inspired by Gustave Moreau's paintings, which Casal viewed in photographic form.

6. Latin American writers in this period were not alone in exploring the art of the Orient. European painters were similarly motivated and inspired by Eastern art forms. Van Gogh in his Paris period used the art of Japanese woodcuts in his work and was an ardent admirer of Hiroshige's canvases. Orientalism was a major element in the formation of modernist hybridity as we shall see in chapter 4.

7. See José Enrique Rodó's essay, *El que vendrá* (The becoming) (11).

8. See his essay "El poema del Niágara" (7: 223–238).

9. Hugh Conway was Frederick John Fargus's pseudonym.

10. The original novel was not published as a single volume but rather as fifteen sections or divisions between the 15th of May and the 15th of September. And Martí did not sign his name to the work but published it under the pseudonym Adelaida Ral. The publisher paid Martí fifty-five dollars, a portion of which he turned over to Adelaida Baralt together with a gallant poem, selected verses of which (translated) read:

> To Adelaida Baralt
> From a novel without excellence
> I send you the commission:
> . . . . . .
> Fifty-five was the amount:
> A fifth is yours: a fifth
> Of fifty-five comes to
> Eleven, if I am not a dullard.
>
> . . . . . .

11. See his remarks on the subject expressed with biting humor (18: 192).

12. Marinetti's work was known by some of the modernists whose compositions postdate the 1909 and 1912 manifestos, and their interest in his proposal was in sync with the modernization of the Latin American economies, the speed of life it produced, the hurried urban movement that some observed, Martí included, in New York, Paris, and the more advanced urban centers of the republics south of the border. Rubén Darío among the modernists read Marinetti and wrote about his aesthetic ideas in an essay entitled "Marinetti and Futurism" (Marinetti y el futurismo) (1950–1953, 1: 616–623).

13. Transpositions of paintings were informed not only by writers in the modernist world but also by painters. In 1889 Van Gogh in St. Remy made colored copies of the works of the great masters, "translating" black and white to color.

14. For the facts about the shipwreck of *L'Amérique* we rely on Henríquez Ureña's colorful recounting of the event in his history of Latin American modernism (152–153).

15. Van Gogh, for example, early in his career, produced copies of Millet's *The Four Hours of the Day*. But he insisted they were not copies: "it is not a copy pure and simple. . . . It is rather *translating* into another language of colors, the impressions of chiaroscuros in white and black" (curator's quotation of Van Gogh at the Museum of Modern Art (New York) exhibit entitled Van Gogh and the Colors of the Night, September 2008). We will return to the question of "translating" art into literature in the case of Casal and Martí.

16. The text should read "Parmigianino," the name by which the Lombard School, high mannerist painter Girolamo Francesco Maria Mazzuoli (1503–1540) was known. He is famous for his long, contorted human forms and was interested in the qualities of grace and perfection such as Silva paints in his portrait of Helen. A figure similar to the Silva translation is Parmigianino's *Madonna of the Long Neck*.

17. We have searched in vain for the painter of the canvas of Silva's Helen. The narrator of the novel says: "Who was the painter. J. F. Siddal whose name is at the bottom of the canvas. . . . Not even the critics who have written

about the Pre-Raphaelite Brotherhood mention him, nor does his name appear in any gallery or museum catalogue" (¿Quién era el pintor, ese J. F. Siddal, cuyo nombre está al pie de la tela. . . . No lo mencionan los críticos que han escrito sobre la Pre-Raphaelite Brotherhood, ni figura su nombre en ninguna galleria, ni catálogo de museo) (163).

18. James Abbot McNeill Whistler (1834–1903), an American-born British-based artist.

19. This diary was popular among the modernists, and references to it appear in several texts of the period in Latin America.

CHAPTER 3. FROM PAINTING TO LITERARY TEXT

1. The full text is cited from my edition of *Versos libres* (Barcelona: Labor, 1970), 60–63. We reproduce the full text in the addendum to this chapter followed by the English translation.

2. Citations of Martí's works come from two sources: the Trópico edition (1936–1953), 74 vols., and the Editorial Nacional edition (1963–1973), 28 vols. The citations of "Pollice verso" come from I. A. Schulman's edition of *Versos libres* (Barcelona: Labor, 1970). The full text of "Pollice verso" and an English translation are given in an addendum at the end of this chapter.

3. We will also examine Poem XXI of his *Versos sencillos*.

4. Martí was an avid art critic and visited galleries regularly in New York and abroad.

5. Dr. Saulo Antonio Fernández (a faculty member of the Instituto Superior Pedagógico "José Martí" de Camagüey, Cuba) in his study (sent to me via the internet) entitled "Metodología para la apreciación del cuadro figurativo, desde la crítica martiana," states that Martí's transpositions are characterized by a "critical-positivistic orientation" (orientación-crítico-positivista, 59).

6. A reference to the repugnant aspects of modern life he observed in New York City.

7. The essay is entitled "Cartas de Verano; II La Universidad de los pobres." This essay, published in *El Partido Liberal*, is not in the *Obras completas* (Editorial Nacional) but was collected and published by Ernesto Mejía Sánchez in his *Nuevas cartas de Nueva York* (Mexico: Siglo XXI, 1980), 156–165.

8. We wish to thank Saulo Antonio Fernández for pointing out the genesis of the poem in his unpublished essay ("Génesis de un poema eterno III: El cuadro inadvertido"), which he kindly made available to me. Many of my comments in this section of the chapter are based upon Fernández's sensitive criticism. The original research on Cazin was published by Professor Fernández in *Islas* 120 and 136 (April–June 1999) and (April–June 2003).

9. Painterly techniques and plastic visualizations abound in Martí's poetry. See, for example, the prologue to his first volume of poetry, *Ismaelillo*, in which

he states with respect to the vision of his son who has inspired his poetry: "When I've stopped seeing you in any form, I've stopped *painting* you" (Cuando he cesado de verte en una forma, he cesado de pintarte). Or, another notable example that underscores how intense Martí's painterly interest is can be found in Poem XXIV of *Versos sencillos*, in which there is a narrative in three stanzas, each about three different painters, their palettes, and themes.

10. See Montero (iii). Moreau's later works, those he began to exhibit in the Salon of 1876, captured the imagination of Casal. Moreau's paintings *Salomé*, *Hercules*, and the *Hydra of Leme* electrified art critics and audiences and established the style by which Moreau came to be known to the public. These works demonstrate a strong leaning toward allegory. And their allusions to unconscious desires and dreams established Moreau as a forerunner to the surrealists. Casal's transpositions are more than mere "positivistic" renderings of the original canvases.

11. Oscar Montero's book, *Erotismo y representación en Julián del Casal*, is the first detailed examination of Casal's prose and poetry and the role eroticism played in his literary production.

12. Montero, relying upon Glickman's research, states that subsequent to the publication of "Salomé" the Cuban wrote to Moreau who then supplied him with copies of his canvases (124).

13. In various previous essays we have studied the case of the Mexican poet, Manuel Gutiérrez Nájera, whose poem "De blanco" (On white) comes close to the Parnassian ideal of impassivity but fails to adhere to the canonical ideal of the Parnassians.

14. Prior to the publication of Montero's seminal analysis of the erotic/gay substrata of his writing, I insisted on going against the grain in an essay in which I floated the idea of a social/political interpretation of the sonnets. See Schulman, "*La Salomé* de Julián del Casal y Guillermo Valencia: *Transposición y werden*," in *Estudios: Edición en homenaje a Guillermo Valencia* (Cali: Carvajal, 1976), 69–84; and Schulman, "Casal's Cuban Counterpoint of Art and Reality," *Latin American Research Review* 11, 2 (1976): 113–128.

15. These were made available in "complete" form in the centenary edition of three volumes published in Cuba in 1963.

16. On this subject, see Vitier's classic book *Lo cubano en la poesía*, Octava Lección.

CHAPTER 4. FACING THE ORIENT

1. All translations from the Spanish are mine.

2. Kabbani observes that the traveler in travel literature "travels to exercise power over land, women, peoples. It is a commonplace of Orientalism that the West knows more about the East than the East knows about itself; this implies a predetermined discourse, however, which limits and in many ways

victimises the Western observer. It is as if the imagination of the traveler, in order to function, has to be sustained by a long tradition of Western scholarship, by other Western texts" (10). Thus the Orient is often reduced to a cliché.

3. Charnon-Deutsch borrows the term *ethnographic alibi* from Mark Alloula, *The Colonial Harem* (Minneapolis: University of Minnesota Press, 1986), 28.

4. Japanese representations of sexual union.

5. For the information on Tablada and his links to the plastic arts I am indebted to Tanabe's informative work.

6. In his prose poem "Japonerías," dedicated to María Cay, Casal wrote: "this morning, upon leaving to take a walk, I saw a Japanese vase worthy of decorating your white bedroom where the footsteps of your admirers or the sonorous echo of sensuous kisses never were heard, oh spiritual María!" (he visto esta mañana, al salir de paseo, un búcaro japonés digno de figurar en tu alcoba blanca ¡oh spiritual María! donde no se han oído nunca las pisadas de tus admiradores o el eco sonoro de los besos sensuales) (145).

CHAPTER 5. WRITERS AS ART CRITICS

1. The best source for studying Martí's art criticism is the definitive work on the subject written by Adelaida De Juan in 1997: *José Martí: Imagen, crítica y mercado de arte*. For a briefer commentary on Martí's art criticism followed by a selection of his ideas on art, see the section on art (274–281) in Martí, *Esquema ideológico de José Martí*, ed. Manuel Pedro Gónzalez and Ivan A. Schulman (Mexico: Cultura, 1961).

2. The first Goya piece is in the form of notes left by Martí in a notebook during his exile period in Madrid.

3. The first version of the Madrazo essay was written in French, also in 1879, and served as the basis of Martí's essay on the Spanish painter published in New York in *The Hour*.

4. Enrique Collazo, an artist friend, spoke to the editors about Martí's talents as an art critic, and they in turn invited Martí to contribute to their magazine. Martí described the contact as follows: "Collazo spoke about me in "The Hour." And here I was with two passes to visit museums,—on my way to the collections of Mr. Stebbins and Wolfes [*sic*], and engaged to write a critical review in English." (Collazo habló de mí en "Th Hour." Y héme, con dos papeletas para ver Museos,—camino de la colección de Mr. Stebbins y de Wolfes, y obligado a hacer de ellos una revista crítica en ingles.) (22: 284).

5. In the sentence immediately following he recommends to Tedín (who is in Paris) that he view in the Louvre paintings by Murillo, and writes that he, in the meantime, thinking of his friend, will be going to see Millet's *Angelus* (7: 396).

6. The challenge is to those painters Martí classifies as "relamidos"—that is, affected in their techniques.

7. The essay was sent to the prestigious Buenos Aires periodical *La Nación*. Martí also wrote about the painting of another principal European artist of his time, the German-Hungarian Mihály Munkákcsy.

8. In an essay sent in 1885 to *La Nación* of Buenos Aires he was severely critical of American art, which he found false in coloration and crude in execution (10: 228). And he noted further that it would be difficult for American art to show truly original qualities when the nature of its society was undefined and in a state of flux. With respect to American art, what is astonishing in this essay is how well acquainted the Cuban was with the major artists of the time whose work he was able to describe briefly and compare with that of Mexican or European masters: Chase, Swain Gifford, Sargent, Quartley, Brown (10: 228–231).

9. This evolutionary or transformational quality of his style and ideas reflects the evolutionary environment of modernity of which he is a product. But it makes the task of pinning down his ideas or the nature of his style—in constant flux—a difficult but at the same time challenging and creative task.

10. Martí's view of the United States is ambivalent—sometimes positive, other times, negative. But as the years advanced, toward the end of the eighties, his opinion of the United States, its politics, its culture, its materialism, led him to adopt a fundamentally negative point of view.

11. Ed. Baschet, Librairie Leon Vanier, Paris. Martí provides no date of publication (19: 321).

12. Goupil & Cie was established in 1850 in Paris by Goupil. His company established worldwide trade of photographic and heliographic reproductions of paintings and sculptures, a fact to which Darío alludes in his essay. Photography, as noted at the outset of this study, permitted the development of reproductive art, and Goupil was a leader in this endeavor with his Ateliers Photographiques, established in the north of Paris in 1869.

13. This was particularly true in the case of many writers. Casal, for example, never managed to travel to Paris, yet he was inspired by the works of the contemporary French artist Gustave Moreau, whose canvases he studied in reproductions.

14. See among his short stories in *Azul* . . . "El rey burgués; cuento alegre."

15. See Martí's essay "El prólogo al *Poema del Niágara*."

16. In his essay "Los poetas modernistas en el mercado económico."

17. Darío only mentions the last name. But a consultation of Goupil's reproductions in the *Tesoro de artes modernas*, held in the Rare Book Room of the University of Illinois, yielded the full name of the artist and the title of the canvas, *Corrida de toros en un circo romano*. We have every reason to believe that Darío consulted this volume in writing his essay "Goupil; El tesoro de artes modernas" (1950–1953, 1: 631–639).

18. Pica (1883–1903) was a Neapolitan critic of literature and art and the first to introduce Japanese art in Italy, where, unlike in France, Britain, and the United States, it was not well known. His interest had its origins in his

admiration for Edmond de Goncourt, who wrote a book on Utamaro in 1891. Pica, three years later, produced *L'arte dell Estremo Oriente*.

19. See our comments in the section that follows.

20. Fernand Khnopff, a Belgian painter, 1858–1921.

21. Henri Evenepoel, a fauvist Belgian painter, 1872–1899.

22. Gaston La Touche (1854–1913). A French self-taught artist who began to paint in 1880 in the seventeenth-century Dutch style. But, by 1890 he discarded his early style and moved in the direction of the colors and light of the impressionists. Today he is classified as a postimpressionist.

23. Tablada speaks of the Parisian vogue for Oriental art and confesses that the study of Japanese art has been an unending fascination for him (1988, 125–126).

CHAPTER 6. AN EPILOGUE AND CONCLUSION: WORDS THAT CREATE OBJECTS

1. See ideas expressed in the introduction and chapter 1, ideas that with regard to the meaning of modernism and its development and presence after the nineteenth century, I have expressed in my previous and ongoing research, which is detailed in the list of works cited. The reader who wishes to explore this subject should consult, in particular, Schulman (2002, chapter 1).

2. See Schulman (2005, 9–25). See also Paz, Rama, and Zavala.

3. Max Henríquez Ureña, the classic historiographer of modernism in his *Breve historia del modernismo* includes Huidobro (1893–1948) among the modernists of Chile but notes that he adopted vanguard forms of literary expression within the *creacionista* movement, which he founded in his later poetry (363).

4. Critics such as Octavio Paz maintain that in modernist writing there is a duality of movement—forward in time and back in time—so that the past is constantly rediscovered and becomes a new future. That is why I believe that it *is* indeed reasonable to think aspects of modernist writing incorporate the counterdiscourses of the past. I believe with Zavala (*Colonialism and Culture*) that there is a relationship between past and present, which in the broadest terms argues in favor of the presence of the subaltern voice in Hispanic literature from the colonial period forward, a voice, however, which with the advent of modernist writing strikes a more forceful and independent presence. On this subject the reader may also wish to consult Fernando Burgos, *Vertientes de la modernidad hispano-americana*.

5. The French poet Guillaume Apollinaire cultivated the poetic calligramme. His poem evoking the Eiffel Tower has the characteristic form of the calligramme.

6. For the Spanish quotes offered in this chapter we will dispense with the translation into English since it is the physical construction of the poem as object that is of primary interest.

7. (1885–1941).

BIBLIOGRAPHY

Aching, Gerard. 1997. *The Politics of Spanish American "Modernismo": By Exquisite Design*. Cambridge: Cambridge University Press.

Adorno, Theodor W. 1973. *Crítica cultural y sociedad*. Barcelona: Ariel.

Ashcroft, B., G. Griffins, and H. Tiffen. 1989. *The Empire Writes Back: Theory and Practice in Post-Colonial Literatures*. London: Routledge.

Azougarth, Abdeslam. 1998. "Martí orientalista." *Casa de las Américas* 210: 12–20.

Barthes, Roland. 1968. *Writing Degree Zero*. New York: Hill and Wang.

Behdad, Ali. 1994. *Belated Travelers: Orientalism in the Age of Colonial Dissolution*. Durham: Duke University Press, 1994.

Bongie, Chris. 1991. *Exotic Memories: Literature, Colonialism, and the Fin de Siècle*. Stanford: Stanford University Press.

Burgos, Fernando. 1995. *Vertientes de la modernidad hispano-americana*. Caracas: Monte Avila.

Calinescu, Matei. 1987. *Five Faces of Modernity: Modernism, Avant-Garde, Decadence, Kitsch, Postmodernism*. Durham: Duke University Press.

Casal, Julián. 1945. *Poesías completas*. Havana: Ministerio de Educación.

———. 1993. *Poesías completas y pequeños poemas en prosa en orden cronológico*. Miami: Ediciones Universal.

Charnon-Deutsch, Lou. 1995. "Exoticism and the Politics of Differences in Late Nineteenth-Century Spanish Periodicals." In *Culture and Gender in Nineteenth-Century Spain*. Oxford: Clarendon.

Clark de Lara, Belem, and Ana Laura Zavala Díaz, eds. 2002. *La construcción del modernismo*. Mexico: Universidad Nacional Autónoma de México, 2002.

Collier, P., and R. Lethbridge, eds. 1944. *Artistic Relations: Literature and the Visual Arts in Nineteenth-Century France*. New Haven: Yale University Press.

Dallmayr, Fred R. 1996. *Beyond Orientalism: Essays on Cross-Cultural Encounter*. Albany: State University of New York Press.

Darío, Rubén. 1950–1953. *Obras completas.* 5 vols. Madrid: Afrodísio Aguado.

―――. 1950–1953. "Narciso Tondreau." In *Obras completas,* vol. 2, 47–64.

―――. 2002. *Cartas desconocidas.* Managua: Fundación Vida.

Dávila, Luis Ricardo. 2009. *Modernidad iberoamericana: cultura, política y cambio social.* Madrid: Vervuert, 2009.

De Juan, Adelaida. 1996. *Pintar como el sol pinta.* Havana: Unión.

―――. 1997. *José Martí: imagen, crítica y mercado de arte.* Havana: Letras Cubanas.

Duby, Georges. 1999. "La historia cultural." In *Para una historia intelectual,* ed. Jean-Pierre Rioux and Jean-François Sirnelli. Mexico: Taurus.

Faber, Sebastian. 2002. "The Beautiful, the Good and the Natural: Martí and the Ills of Modernity." *Journal of Latin American Cultural Studies* 11, 2: 173–193.

Fountain, Anne. 2003. *José Martí and U.S. Writers.* Gainesville: University of Florida Press.

Frascina, Francis, Tamar Garb, Nigel Blake, Charles Harrison, and Briony Fer. 1993. *Modernity and Modernism in French Painting in the Nineteenth Century.* New Haven: Yale University Press.

Freedman, Ralph. 1963. *The Lyrical Novel.* Princeton: Princeton University Press, 1963.

García Marruz, Fina. 2001. *Darío, Martí y lo germinal americano.* Havana: Ediciones UNION.

Garfield, Evelyn Picon, and Ivan A. Schulman. 1991. *Contextos: Literatura y sociedad latinos americanas del siglo XIX.* Urbana and Chicago: University of Illinois Press.

―――, eds. 1999. *Poesía modernisa: Antología.* 2nd ed. San Juan: Editorial de la Universidad de Puerto Rico.

Giordano, Jaime. 1985. *La edad de la náusea.* Santiago de Chile: Universidad Profesional del Pacífico.

Goic, Cedomil. 2003. "Bibliografía de y sobre Vicente Huidobro." *Anales de la literatira chilena* 2: 317–319.

Gomáriz, José. 1995. *Colinialismo e independencia cultural.* Madrid: Verbum.

Gómez Carrillo, Enrique. 1954. *Páginas escogidas.* Guatemala: Biblioteca de la Cultura Popular.

González, Aníbal. 1987. *La novela modernista* hispanoamericana. Madrid: Gredos, 1987.

Gonzalez, Echeverría Roberto. 1980. "Modernidad, modernismo y nueva narrativa: El recurso del metodo." *Revista Interamerican de Bibliografía* 2: 157–163.

Gullón, Ricardo. 1953. *El modernismo: notas de un curso.* Mexico: Aguilar.

―――. 1964. *Direcciones del modernismo.* Madrid: Gredos.

Gutiérrez Nájera, Manuel. 2000. *Poesía.* Ed. Angel Muñõz Fernández. Mexico: Factoría Ediciones.

Herrera y Reissig, Julio. 1942. *Poesías completas.* Buenos Aires: Losada.

Herut, Syrene-Chafic. 1997. *Viewing Europe from the Outside: Cultural Encounters and Critiques in the Eighteenth-Century Pseudo-Oriental Travelogue and the Nineteenth-Century 'Voyage en Orient.'* New York: Lang.

Hidalgo Paz, Ibrahim. 2007. *Martí en España, España en Martí (1871–1874).* Havana: Centro de Estudios Martianos.

Hutcheon, Linda. 1986–1987. "Postmodern Paratextuality and History." *Texte* 5, 6: 301–312.

Jacobs, Karen. 2001. *The Eye's Mind: Literary Modernism and Visual Culture.* Ithaca: Cornell University Press.

Jiménez, José Olivio. 1983. *José Martí, poesía y existencia.* Mexico: Oasis.

Jiménez, Juan Ramón. 1962 [1953]. *El modernismo: Notas de un curso.* Mexico: Aguilar.

Johnson, Paul. 1991. *The Birth of the Modern: World Society 1815–1830.* New York: Harper Collins.

Jrade, Cathy L. 1998. *Modernism, Modernity and the Development of Spanish American Literature.* Austin: University of Texas Press.

Juan-Navarro, Santiago. 2000. *Archival Reflections: Postmodern Fiction of the Americas.* Lewisburg: Bucknell University Press.

Kabbani, Rana. 1986. *Europe's Myths of the Orient.* Bloomington: Indiana University Press.

Knight, Christopher. 2010. "Art Review: 'The Spectacular Art of Jean-Léon Gérôme' @ J. Paul Getty Museum." *Los Angeles Times.* http://latimesblogs. latimes.com/culturemonster/2010/06/art-review-the-spectacular-art-of-j-paul-getty-museum.html.

Kushigian, Julia Alexis. 1991. *Orientalism in the Hispanic Literary Tradition: In Dialogue with Borges, Paz, and Sarduy.* Albuquerque: University of New Mexico Press.

Lozano Herrera, Rubén. 2001. *Las versa y las burlas de José Juan Tablada.* Mexico: Universidad Iberoamericana.

Lugones, Leopoldo. 2959. *Obras poéticas completas.* Madrid: Aguilar.

Malculuzynski, M-Pierrette. 1991. *Sociocríticas, practices, cultura de fronteras.* Amsterdam: Rodopi.

Meltzer, Françoise. 1987. *Salomé and the Dance of Writing.* Chicago: University of Chicago Press.

Marinello, Juan. 2000. *Martí en 15 esferas estelares.* Mérida: Cátedras martianas de José Martí.

Martí, José. 1936–1953. *Obras de Martí.* 74 vols. Havana: Trópico.

———. 1961. *Esquema ideológico.* Ed. Manuel Pedro Gónzalez and Ivan A. Schulman. Mexico: Cultura.

———. 1963–1978. *Obras completas.* 28 vols. Havana: Editorial Nacional.

———. 1993. *Epistolario.* 3 vols. Havana: Editorial de Ciencias Sociales.

———. 2000. *Lucía Jerez.* Ed. Mauricio Núñez. Havana: Centro de Estudios Martianos.

———. 2002. *Selected Writings*. Ed. Esther Allen. New York: Penguin Books.

———. 2005. *Lucía Jerez*. Ed. Ivan A. Schulman. Buenos Aires: Stockcero.

———. 1990. "Pollice verso" (Thumbs down). Trans. Jo Anne Engelbert. Unpublished manuscript.

Martínez, Mayra Beatriz. 2005. *Martí, eros y mujer*. Havana: Pinos Nuevos.

McHale, Brian. 1988. "Change of Dominant from Modernist to Postmodernist Writing." In *Postmodern Fiction in Europe and the Americas*, 53–79. Amsterdam: Rodopi.

Montero, Oscar. 1993. *Erotismo y representación en Julián del Casal*. Amsterdam: Rodopi.

Nervo, Amado. 1962. *Obras completas*. Madrid: Aguilar.

Onís, Federico de. 1955. *España en América*. Madrid: Ediciones de la Universidad de Puerto Rico.

Payeras Grau, María, and Luis Migue Fernández Ripoll, eds. 2001. *Fine(es) del siglo y modernismo*. Universitat de les Illes Balears.

Paz, Octavio. 1965a. "Estela de José Juan Tablada." *Las peras del olmo*, 80–89. Mexico: Universidad Nacional Autónoma, 1965.

———. 1965b. *Cuadrivio*. Mexico: J. Mortiz.

———. 1974. *Los hijos del limo: del romanticismo a la vanguardia*. Barcelona: Seix Barral.

Praz, Mario. 1975. *Mnemosyne: The Parallel between Literature and the Visual Arts*. Princeton: Princeton University Press.

Rama, Angel. 1967. *Los poetas modernistas en el Mercado económico*. Montevideo: Universidad de la República, Facultad de Humanidades y Ciencias.

———. 1974. "La dialéctica de la modernidad en José Martí." *Estudios Martianos*, 129–174. San Juan: Universidad de Puerto Rico.

Real de Azúa, Carlos. 1950. "Ambiente espiritual del novecientos." *Número* (January–February): 15–36.

Rebolledo, Efrén. 1968. *Obras completas*. Ed. Luis Mario Schneider. México: Ediciones de Bellas Artes.

Rodó, José Enrique. 1920. *El que vendrá*. Barcelona: Editorial Cervantes.

Rothker, Susana. 1992. *Fundación de una escritura*. Havana: Casa de las Américas.

Said, Edward W. 1978. *Orientalism*. New York: Pantheon Books.

Santiáñez, Nil. 2000. *Investigaciiones literarias: Modernidad, historia de la literatura y modernismos*. Barcelona: Editorial Crítica.

Schulman, Ivan. 1966. *Génesis del modernismo*. Mexico: El Colegio de México.

———. 1981. "Modernismo/Modernidad: Apostillas a la teoría de la Edad Moderna." In *In Honor of Boyd G. Carter*, 105–113. Laramie: University of Wyoming Press.

———. 1986. "Las genealogías secretas de la narrativa: del modernismo a la vanguardia hispánica." In *La prosa de la vanguardia hispánica*, 153–175. Madrid: Orígenes.

———. 1987. "Modernismo/Modernidad: Metamorfósis de un concepto." Introduction to *Nuevos asedios al modernismo*, 11–38. Madrid: Editorial Taurus.

————. 1998. "Modernismo/Modernidad y el proyecto de alzar la nación." *Journal of Iberian and Latin American Studies* 4: 121–132.

————. 2002. *El proyecto inconcluso: la vigencia del modernismo*. Mexico: Siglo Veintiuno.

————. 2005. *Vigencias: Martí y el modernismo*. Havana: Centro de Estudios Martianos.

————, and Evelyn Picon Garfield. 1984. "Las entrañas del vacío." In *Ensayos sobre la modernidad hispanoamericana*. Mexico: Cuadernos Americanos.

Scott, David. *Artistic Relations: Literature and the Visual Arts in Nineteenth-Century France*. New Haven: Yale University Press, 1994.

Silva, José Asunción. 1996. *De sobremesa*. Introduction by Gabriel García Márquez. Madrid: Hiperión.

Sinor, Denis. 1954. *Orientalism and History*. Cambridge: W. Heffer.

Spivak, Gayatri Chakravorty. 1996. *The Spivak Reader: Selected Works of Gayatri Chakravorty Spivak*, ed. Donna Landry and Gerald MacLean. New York: Routledge.

Tablada, José Juan. 1899. *El florilegio*. Mexico: Imprenta de Ignacio Escalante.

————. 1904. *El florilegio*. Introduction by Jesús E. Valenzuela. Mexico: Librería de la Viuda de Ch. Bouret.

————. 1953. *Los mejores poemas de José Juan Tablada*. Selección y prólogo de J. M. González de Mendoza. Mexico: Editorial Surco.

————. 1971. *Obras I*. Mexico: Universidad Nacional Autónoma de México.

————. 1988. *Obras III*. Mexico: Universidad Nacional Autónoma de México.

————. 2006. *En el pías del sol*. Edited by Jorge Ruedas.

Tanabe, Atsuko. 1981. *El japonismo de José Juan Tablada*. Mexico: Universidad Nacional Autónoma de México.

Tiffin, Chris, and Alan Lawson, eds. 1994. *De-scribing Empire: Post-Colonialism and Texuality*. New York: Routledge.

Tinajero, Araceli. 2004. *Orientalismo en el modernismo hispanoamericano*. West Lafayette: Purdue University Press.

Touraine, Alain. 1994. *Crítica de la modernidad*. Mexico: Fondo de Cultura Económica.

Turner, Bryan S. 1994. *Orientalism, Postmodernism, and Globalism*. London: Routledge.

Valencia, Guillermo. 1955. *Obras poéticas completas*. Madrid: Aguilar.

Vitier, Cintio. 1970. *Lo cubano en la poesía*. Havana: Instituto del Libro.

Yegenoglu, Meyda. 1998. *Colonial Fantasies: Towards a Feminist Reading of Orientalism*. Cambridge: Cambridge University Press.

Young, Robert. 1990. *White Mythologies: Writing History and the West*. New York: Routledge.

Ward, Patricia A., and James S. Patty. 2001. *Baudelaire and the Poetics of Modernity*. Nashville: Vanderbilt University Press.

Zavala, Iris M. 1992. *Colonialism and Culture: Hispanic Modernism and the Social Imaginary*. Bloomington: Indiana University Press.

INDEX